Your Response
Could Make
A Difference!!

Your Response Could Make A Difference!!

By

DR. DAVID AJETGBE

ARPress
ILLUMINATING IDEAS
EMPOWERING VOICES

ARPress
45 Dan Road Suite 36
Canton MA 02021
Hotline: 1(888) 821-0229
Fax: 1(508) 545-7580

Ordering Information:
Quantity Sales. Special discounts are available on quantity purchases by corporations, associations, and others. For details, contact the publisher at the address above.

Printed in the United States of America.

ISBN-13   Paperback   979-8-89676-601-8
                eBook   979-8-89676-602-5

Library of Congress Control Number: 2024901755

Table of Contents

Introduction..1

Goal of the Book...2

Adam and Eve...3

Response of Cain..8

Noah Built an Ark in Response to God 11

Abraham and Lot...18

Abraham's Response to God 19

Isaac and Rebecca...23

Laban and Jacob..25

Departure of Jacob from Laban 27

Jacob Met Esau..29

Response of Joseph's Brothers 32

Joseph and Potiphar's Wife...................................34

Joseph in Prison 36

Joseph Response to his Brothers 40

Joseph Met Benjamin and his brothers 45

Joseph Revealed Himself to His Brothers............50

Egyptians Response to the Israelites...................54

Moses Response to God 57

Pharaoh's Response 59

The Plagues in Egypt 61

The Golden Calf..65

Moses Responded to God in a Plea......................66

Moses and Joshua, Puzzled 67

Moses Responded in Anger 68

A Journey of 40 Days took 14,610 Days 71

Falling of the Wall of Jericho 80

Daniel in the King's Palace in Babylon 82

Daniel and the King's Dream 84

Shadrach, Meshach, and Abednego in the burning furnace 86

Shadrach, Meshach, and Abednego in the
   Fierce Burning Furnace 88

Daniel in the Den of Lions....................................90

Saul's Response and the
loss of his Kingship..93
David and Saul..95
Nathan Confronted David 102
David's Response to the Return of the Ark of Covenant..........106
Hannah's Response..108
Consequences of Rehoboam's Response 110
Effects of Ruth's Response to the Tragedy in Her Life 114
The Widow and the Prophet....................................119
Effects of Job's Responses 122
Job's Friends Visited him..124
Job's Friends' Attitude...125
Response to a Grieving Person.................................127
Jonah's Response...132
Zachariah's Response to the Angel 136
The Shepherds' Response to Joseph and Mary 138
Satan Tempted Jesus 140
The Woman of Samaria 143
Peter's Response to Fear..146
Jesus' Teaching on Ways to Respond........................150
The Unforgiving Servant 153
Invitation to the Wedding Feast 160
Response of the Ten Virgins 163
The Rich man and the Kingdom of God 166
Response of The Rich Fool 168
The Ten Talents 170
Arrest of Jesus..173
Peter Cut the Servants Ear Off 174
Jesus Response at His Crucifixion............................178
Response of the Thieves...180
Judas Iscariot's Response to his Betrayal of Jesus 181
Responses of Ananias and Sapphira 185
Response to Conflict Between Believers....................187
Response of Stephen at His Stoning 189
Paul and Silas Responses to their Imprisonment......191
Response to Thorn in the Flesh 196
Response to Nagging Emotional Irritants 198

Children in the Family 205
Response to Middle Child.....................................208
Response to 'Front Seat Passenger Driver'................210
Effects of Outside Issues on Family Responses.........212
Responses at Work 215
Response to Someone 'Picking a Fight' with You......219
Response to Those in Power over You 221
Gossiping 224
Responses Elicited by 'WHY' 227
Response to Disappoinment..................................233
Response to Flexibility..240

Introduction

Response is the backbone of all human relationships to situations and issues, to other humans, and to God. The outcomes are the results of varying responses which could be positive or negative outcomes, but all depend on the responses. Humans face several issues daily requiring a variety of responses. However, the type or the manner of response depends on the individual and the situations. Each person responds to situations and issues in his or her own learned or conditioned manner. Those responses vary from positive to negative, accommodation to rejection, love to hate, friendship to enmity, understanding to indifference, forgiveness to revenge, being humane to being non-humane, giving 'benefits of the doubt' to giving no allowance to other possibilities, and other shades of responses which one could imagine. However, the Bible is emphatic in saying that "Therefore if anyone is in Christ, this person is a new creation; the old things have passed away; behold, new things have come" (2 Corinthians 5: 17, NASB). With this statement God expects Christians to become new after accepting Christ, the old ways of behavior are old and just as an old cloth is discarded old behavior must be discarded which include a way of responding to issues/situations before one becomes a Christian. Human responses to issues are old, inadequate, and Christ's way of response should be allowed to take over.

Goal of the Book

This book will reveal examples of how in the Bible individuals, groups, and national leaders responded to the relationships, instructions, or requests from God. It will also show the consequences of their responses and provide a lesson on the appropriate ways to respond to issues and demands as they present themselves. This book will point to examples of responses and consequences which are Important to be familiar with in the word of God This book will show examples of the importance of being knowledgeable and having in depth understanding of the Bible to have appropriate responses to temptations and issues in individuals' lives. It was the knowledge of the Bible which Christ used to confront the devil when He was being tempted. Jesus was able to counter and respond more appropriately and vended off satan by using the word of God. As a result of this example the followers of God should make it a point of their being to read the Bible regularly. One of the goals of this book is to encourage those who have formed the habits of reading the Bible to increase their practice. This book is also to encourage those who have not been reading the Bible to begin the habit of reading it. This book intends to direct readers to follow Christ's example in responding to issues in such ways that would honor Him and follow His directions. Another goal of the book is to show the importance of following God, submitting to God, and respecting others thus serving as true representative of God.

Adam and Eve

Going back to the beginning of creation God provided a safe living environment for Adam and Eve and gave them opportunities to live freely. God gave them only one major responsibility or command and that was for them to have nothing to do with the tree in the middle of the garden, but they had freedom to everything else in the garden.

As time went by, they continually received God's regular daily visit. On one occasion the devil visited too. Adam's and Eve's responses to the devil were dismal. Instead of shunning away the devil they accommodated him.

"Submit therefore to God. But resist the devil, and he will flee from you" (James 4 - 7, NASB). Their responses to the devil changed everything in their relationship with God and in God's response to them.

Just because they responded favorably to the devil, he was able to have his ways with them. The devil was encouraged to pursue his deceitful and evil plan with them. The devil was able to misrepresent God before them. Knowing what God has done for them and His companionship and visit to them daily should have made them know better and they should have had a measured response to the devil, but they did not. They allowed their selfishness to override a better response to the devil without considering their knowledge of God through His relationship with them.

Not only did they succumb to the devil's devices, but they ruined their relationship with God and with each other also.

They started blaming each other. Adam was very defensive in his response to God by accusing God when he said, "the woman you gave me gave me the fruit" (Genesis 3: 12, NASB).

Instead of taking responsibility for his own action he blamed God for giving him the wife - Eve. Since Adam received the instruction directly from God not to eat the fruit from a particular tree in the middle of the garden with the consequence of dying for disobedience, he was in a good position to intervene when the devil was deceiving them, however, he was just standing there soaking everything in and imagining how good things would be for them by eating the fruit which God forbade them from eating. Adam's response of elation of becoming like God and being a willing participant in disobeying God's command brought God's wrath and curse on him. When Adam was caught, his first response was to blame God and then to blame his wife - Eve. Adam's response was to take no responsibility for his actions and for the actions of his wife - Eve. Not only did he not take responsibility, but his response was to punt the responsibility to others, first to God and then to Eve. His wife, Eve, did not take responsibility, as well. Instead for Eve to ask God for forgiveness she punted the responsibility and fault to the devil. It is an innate human tendency to crave to do what humans are told not to do.

Without looking too far one could see the example with the speed limit. If people will be truthful there are fewer drivers who always adhere to the speed limit. Humans, in general would give excuses for doing the wrong thing. Majority of drivers do not observe the speed limit except when there is/are law enforcement officer(s) close by. Human response is doing all with which he/she could get away with, without being caught. This strategy works most of the time when dealing with another human being, however, it does not work when dealing with God. When dealing with God, the only way to get out of trouble is to confess the sin and ask God for forgiveness. After being forgiven God expects an individual to turn one hundred and eighty degrees (180 degrees) away from the sin. Paul declared emphatically and said "What shall we say then? Shall we go on sinning so that grace may increase? By no means! We are those who have died to sin; how can we live in it any longer?" (Roman 6: 1 - 2 - NASB). In the case of Adam and Eve they did not show any remorse for their sins, they neither confessed nor asked God for forgiveness. From their lack of contrite, they remained in sin and the grace they enjoyed up to that point ended and they were driven out of the garden of Eden. We will continue to wonder what would have happened if Adam's response was of taking responsibility for his actions and for the actions of Eve, his wife. Could God have forgiven them instead of punishing them, could they have been able to continue to enjoy the companionship of God and His daily visit!

If their responses had been of remorse what difference could have God's responses to their sins be! Could God have allowed them to stay in the garden of Eden and enjoy the daily free provisions which they have been enjoying since God created them! However, due to their responses of non-contrite, God drove them out of the garden of Eden. Adam and Eve were denied the 'free lunch' they have been accustomed to receiving while in the garden of Eden during the time they kept God's commandment. However, since their action was to listen to the voice of the devil the consequence was for them to leave the garden of Eden, to work hard for their livelihood tilling the soil which had been cursed because of their sins. The soil being cursed resulted in the soil's fertility being reduced and its productivity being reduced resulting in poor crop yield. Reduction in soil productivity resulted in Adam having to work extremely hard and long before he was able to have enough food for himself, his wife, and even his descendants to eat. Eve's response did not go without punishment, God made it not to be easy for Eve to give birth to children as of that time onward, but it would be through pain, suffering, and discomfort as perpetual punishments which was transferred to all women as a result of Eve's response to the devil.

Response of Cain

Cain, and Abel were the first twin brothers. Cain was a farmer and Abel was a herdsman. Each of them brought an offering to the Lord. Each of them was to bring the best offering to the Lord and both must have been knowledgeable of that requirement. Cain did not care much about the quality of his offering to the Lord. He brought an offering as if he was forced to do so. He did not give the best that he was able to give, and his offering appeared to be given begrudgingly. The Lord who saw the heart of Cain was aware of what was going on in it. Therefore, the Lord rejected his offering because it was not given with pure motive. Abel, on the other hand sought out the best of his flock and gave it as an offering to the Lord. In the same manner the Lord saw the heart of Abel and knew that he gave with good intentions and a pure heart. The Lord rejected Cain's offering but accepted Abel's offering. This situation created sibling rivalry and Cain was very angry with Abel as if Abel was the Lord, who rejected his offering. Evil intent was creeping into Cain's heart against his brother, Abel. The Lord was aware of Cain's anger against Abel and the Lord said to Cain, your brother did not have anything to do about the rejection of your offering. It was all your responsibility to have brought the right offering to Me, but you failed to do so. If you had brought the offering which I, the Lord, deserved I would have accepted your offering just as I accepted your brother's. The Lord then warned Cain that the devil could take advantage of his anger to do evil against his brother. The Lord knew that no good could happen with an uncontrolled anger and He warned Cain. The Lord warned Cain of the danger of allowing the devil to control him. The Lord told Cain that sin was knocking on his door and to resist it. The Lord was telling him not to give way to the devil and to master his emotion. The Lord in essence was telling Cain not to open the door of his heart to the devil. It was a strong warning from the Lord. But Cain did not adhere to the voice

8

of the Lord, but he allowed his emotions to get 'the best of him' and he killed his brother, Abel, in the field and buried him to hide the evidence. It was only two of them in the field and there was no one else there to witness the killing, therefore, he buried Abel so no one could find the trace of his brother. There was one thing which Cain did not know or realize which was that the Lord was/is everywhere, when no one else was/is. Cain thought he had gotten away with murder. He must have been surprised when the Lord asked; "Where is Abel your brother?" Cain immediately responded in a lie to the Lord and followed it up with a defense by saying, "I do not know. Am I my brother's keeper?" His response indicated his intention to lie about his crime and to question the Lord. In Cains's response he was saying to the Lord, when did it become my responsibility to look out for the welfare of my brother? But Cain's tactic did not work out because the Lord posed a direct question to him, "What have you done?" The Lord followed up with the evidence which was that the voice of Abel's blood was crying out to the Lord from the ground where Cain buried him. Cain's responses and his hard heartedness caused the Lord to curse him. The lord's punishment for Cain was not limited to cursing him, but the ground was cursed too because of the sin of Cain. The land would no longer yield the best crop for Cain. Another punishment on Cain was that he would be a nomad, he would not have a place to call his own because he would become a wanderer and a drifter on the earth. Cain immediately felt the weight of his punishment and he was concerned that he would not be able to bear it. Then Cain recounted the punishment placed on him because of his actions. He was not repentant of his sin, but he was so self-centered that all he could think about was himself and his punishments. He did not show any remorse for killing his brother without a cause, but his focus was on himself thinking that someone might kill him. It was ironic that the one who killed his brother did not want to be killed by someone else. He valued his own life more than he valued the life of his brother to whom he showed no mercy. He complained to the Lord about his punishments instead of confessing to the Lord of his sin. However, he said whoever finds me will kill me. The Lord was or is slow to anger and plentiful in mercy, therefore, the Lord protected him from anyone who could

9

have killed him by putting a mark on him so that no one would attempt to kill him. (Genesis 4: 1 - 16, NASB).

Noah Built an Ark in Response to God

The wickedness of humans was very repugnant to God since human thoughts, aspirations and imagination was to do evil, not once, twice, thrice, but continually. Humans were chronic evil doers and violence filled the earth. God wished that He had not created humans on the earth and their behavior grieved Him. Humans were so deep in their evil intent that there was no redemption for them but to eliminate them. God decided to eliminate humans, beast, and the creeping things, and the fowls of the air. God then decided an elimination plan for humans, but in His plan, He decided to save the one (Noah) who had been faithful to Him. Through God's grace He decided to save Noah and his household. Not only did God decide to save Noah, his household, and some representative beasts, the creeping thing, and the fowls of the air, but God assigned Noah with some responsibilities.

God told Noah to build an ark in the middle of the desert where there was no water for the boat to float. Noah's response was an acceptance of the responsibility which God gave him without hesitation or questioning God. He did not use logic, but he responded in faith to God's assignments. The writer of Hebrews acknowledges the faith of Noah by declaring "By faith Noah, being warned by

God about things not yet seen, in reverence prepared an ark for the salvation of his household, by which he condemned the world, and became an heir of the righteousness which is according to faith (Hebrews 11:7, NASB). The first assignment was for Noah to build an ark. God gave Noah the dimensions of the ark and Noah built the ark according to God's directives. "Now behold, I Myself am bringing the flood of water upon the earth, to destroy all flesh in which there is the breath of life, from under heaven; everything that is on the earth shall perish. But I will establish My covenant with you; and you shall enter the ark you, your sons, your wife, and your sons' wives with you "(Genesis 6: 17 – 18). God then told Noah that He intended to destroy the earth with every living being in it with the flood. It was at this time that Noah knew the purpose for the ark which he built, however, before then he was just following God by faith because he did not see what was coming. The second assignment was for Noah to take some creatures with him into the ark to spare their lives.

God gave the directives on how to select the creatures to take with him. "And of every living thing of all flesh, two of every sort shalt thou bring into the ark, to keep them alive with thee; they shall be male and female. Of fowls after their kind, and of cattle after their kind, of every creeping thing of the earth after his kind, two of every sort shall come unto thee, to keep them alive. The third assignment was for Noah to take all kind of food that is eaten with him in the ark for all in the ark to eat for the duration of the flood throughout their encampment in the ark. In response, Noah followed God's directives diligently. (Genesis 6; 5 – 16: 19 -22, NASB). God told Noah to have all his household members enter the ark, then God told him to take seven pairs of every clean beast male and female, and of beasts that are not clean in a pair, the male and his female, seven pairs of fowls of the air male and its female. God then told Noah that there would be flood upon the earth for forty days and forty nights. The water was upon the earth and it lifted the ark up. The water covered the high mountains and trees for one hundred and fifty days. As a result of the flood all living things died including man, fowl, cattle, beasts, and every creeping thing. (Genesis 7: 1 - 24, NASB). God was very merciful unto Noah, and He remembered him and every living thing which was with him in the ark and God stopped the rain from falling and He caused the flood to subside upon the surface of the earth for a period of one hundred and fifty days. In order to check out the condition of the earth Noah sent out a ravine which flew to and from until the waters dried up from the earth.

Then he sent forth a dove out of the ark which did not find a place to land or rest because the water still filled the earth. The dove returned to Noah in the ark. After seven days he sent back the dove to check the water level on the earth.

The dove returned to Noah with an olive leave in its mouth. This signified to Noah that the water has abated from the earth. Noah paused for another seven days and sent the dove back to the earth,

but the dove did not return to him any longer. The fact that the dove did not return was a definite indication to Noah that the water had receded well enough for the dove to find a place to rest and stay, therefore, Noah decided that all living creatures with him including humans were safe to go out of the ark to the land. Noah visualized the land from inside the ark and saw that the land was dry. Although Noah saw that the land was dry and ready to accept humans and all other creatures in the ark with him, but Noah did not want to 'jump the gun' by taking any irrational action without getting directives from God. While he was waiting for God's direction for his next line of action, God told him to get out of the ark with all living Creatures, (Genesis 8:16-19, NASB). In relation to the ark and the redemption of humans and other creatures there are two significant subjects, one is the olive tree or branch, and the other was the dove. The dove represented an object of sacrifice to appease God for human sins. The dove represents the Holy Spirit as an indication of peace between God and humans and a certification of the authenticity of Jesus to the world and the olive tree represents peace. When Noah sent the dove out it was through the direction of God that he sent the dove. The dove is a caring bird unlike the raven which Noah sent at first. The raven never returned to provide Noah with the information Noah needed to make a decision. The raven went on its own way without thinking about Noah who sent it out to gather information for him. The raven did not care. Under God's direction, Noah sent a dove as a representation of the Holy Spirit in its reliability and completeness of purpose. The dove came back with an indication that there was no place for it to rest which was an indication to Noah to 'stay tight' because there was still plenty of flood water on

14

the earth and that it was not good for humans' and other creatures' habitation yet. Noah got the message loud and clear, therefore, he waited a while before sending the dove out of the ark to 'test the water' again. Upon returning this time the dove came back with the tidings of good news which was not only for Noah's family and the creatures in the ark, but for the entire earth. The good news was symbolic in the olive branch or leave with which the dove returned to the ark. The involvement of the dove was a double dose of peace with the fact that the dove represents peace and the olive branch or leaf represents peace. What else could have Noah asked from God besides peace and God knew Noah's heart and he sent him a double dose of peace. The peace which God provided was a prelude of God's future actions as specified in God's promise. "And the LORD smelled a sweet savor; and the LORD said in his heart, I will not again curse the ground any more for man's sake; for the imagination of man's heart is evil from his youth; neither will I again smite any more everything living, as I have done. While the earth remained, seedtime and harvest, and cold and heat, and summer and winter, and day and night shall not cease" (Genesis 8: 21 - 22, NASB). There are several references of the dove as a representation of the object for sacrifice and of the Holy Spirit. As object of sacrifice, it was affordable for poor people to sacrifice as sin or burnt offerings. "But if his offering to the LORD is a burnt offering of birds, then he shall bring his offering from the turtledoves or from young doves" (Leviticus 1: 14, NASB). "'But if he cannot afford a lamb, then he shall bring to the LORD his guilt offering for that in which he has sinned, two turtledoves or two young doves, one as a sin offering and the other as a burnt offering" (Leviticus 5: 7, NASB) "But if his means are insufficient for two turtledoves or two young doves, then for his offering for that which he has sinned, he shall bring the tenth of an ephah of fine flour as a sin offering; he shall not put oil on it or place incense on it, for it is a sin offering" (Leviticus 5: 11, NASB). From the beginning of humankind God has always been concerned about the poor who have little resources to do what are necessary for them to do for the atonement of their sins. God made provision and allowances to accommodate them as seen in the Biblical instruction regarding substitutes for expensive sacrificial animals. God accepted the poor people's offerings or sacrifices using doves. When it comes to human salvation and God's dealings with human beings through the Holy Spirit He portrayed the dove as the messenger of good news. "In the beginning God created the heavens and the earth. And the earth was formless and desolate emptiness, and darkness was over the surface of the deep, and the Spirit of God was hovering over the surface of the waters. (Genesis 1: 1 - 2, NASB). "Now when all the people were baptized, Jesus also was baptized, and while He was praying, heaven was opened, and the Holy Spirit descended upon Him in bodily form like a dove, and a voice came from heaven: "You are My beloved Son, in You I am well pleased" (Luke 3: 22, NASB). " And John testified, saying, "I have seen the Spirit descending as a dove out of heaven, and He remained upon Him" (John 1: 32, NASB). All the Biblical references above likened the dove to the Holy Spirit. The Jewish people accepted the dove as one of the most ancient symbols of God. The Babylonian Talmud associated the Spirit of God with the dove. In Genesis 1: 2, hovering over the water during the creation was associated to a dove. The association was a mirror image of how a dove hovers over her delicate young ones without touching them, but in so doing providing them protection, just as God gently protects His creation. The dove traditionally, in the ancient times became associated with the Spirit of God. Early Christians accepted the dove unquestionably as a depiction of the Holy Spirit. The dove with its white feathers depicts the image of the purity of God without blemish. (Philip Koslowski). The olive branch/ leave carried back by the dove was another symbol of peace. The olive branch was so widely associated with peace that there came about a saying. 'Extend the olive branch.' Looking at the phrase superficially it might not appear to mean much, but a deep look at the phrase would show the deep meaning and intent associated with the phrase. 'Extending an olive branch' means to offer peace to another in an argument, in a fight, during the time of hostility and conflict between individuals or nations (Elissy Felix; Gary Allen; Dominique Dallemagne).

Therefore, the dove returning with the branch or leaf of the olive tree in its mouth was an indication of the end of hostility between God and humans. God through the dove extended peace to Noah.

The extension of the olive branch to humans continued until the death of Christ for the world and it continues after the death of Christ and throughout eternity.

Abraham and Lot

When God directed Abraham to leave his native land to another land which God would show him, Abraham obeyed God. Abraham took his family members and Lot, his nephew with him. The Lord blessed both in the land where God directed them. However, as their prosperities increased so was the need to get larger pastures for their animals to graze. The land to graze for the animals of Abraham and the animals of Lot appeared to be shrinking. As the reality of not having enough pastures for the animals of both sides became diminished so were the controversies between the herdsmen of Abraham and the herdsmen of Lot increased. The controversies between them grew fierce to the point of affecting the relationship between Abraham and Lot. When Abraham noticed that a rift was creeping into his relationship with his nephew, he decided to take a 'higher ground' to preserve their relationship as the uncle to Lot. Abraham felt that maintaining a good relationship with his nephew was more valuable to him than any other material gains. Therefore, he summoned his nephew into a family meeting to resolve the issue before it ruined their relationships. In their conference, Abraham reiterated the issues between the herdsmen of both regarding the grazing land. Abraham made it plainly clear to Lot that he would not allow anything to disrupt their relationships. In the Jewish culture the older has the right to the first choice, therefore, in this case, Abraham, the uncle had the right to first choice, but, for the shake of peace between Abraham and Lot, Abraham decided to relinquish his right of choice. Abraham allowed Lot to make the first choice of the grazing land for his animals. Abraham, by yielding to Lot the right of first choice demonstrated to Lot that his relationship to Lot was more valuable than any material gains and Abraham believed that God would do the best for him. Abraham's response to what could have ended as a terrible situation turned out to reinforce the amicable relationship between the uncle and his nephew.

Abraham's Response to God

As the follower of God one must be prepared for how God might challenge one. It is important to take issues as challenges in order to get the courage to tackle them as they appear. God does not put any challenge/test before humans that is more than what God knows that person could handle. Just as it was the case with Job, God knew his heart and was sure that Job would not deny Him, this was the situation with Abraham, as well. This is because God knows the heart of everyone, and He knows how much challenge an individual could handle. "… God tested Abraham, and told him to offer Isaac, his only son whom he loved so much as a burnt offering to Him on a mountain. Abraham got up early in the morning and saddled his donkey and took two of his young men with him and his son Isaac. Abraham split wood for the burnt offering and set out and went to the place of which God had told him.… I and the boy will go over there; and we will worship and return to you. … Abraham took the wood for the burnt offering and laid it on his son Isaac, and he took in his hand the fire and the knife. So, the two of them walked on together. Isaac spoke to his father Abraham and said, My father!… Look, the fire and the wood, but where is the lamb for the burnt offering? Abraham said, God will provide for Himself the lamb for the burnt offering, my son. So, the two of them walked on together.… Abraham built the altar and arranged the wood and bound his son Isaac and laid him on the altar, on top of the wood. And Abraham reached out with his hand and took the knife to slaughter his son. But the angel of the LORD called to him from heaven and said, Abraham, Abraham! And he said, Here I am. He said, Do not reach out your hand against the boy, and do not do anything to him; for now I know that you fear God, since you have not withheld your son, your only son, from Me. Then Abraham raised his eyes and looked, and behold, behind him was a ram caught in the thicket by its horns; and Abraham went and took the ram and offered it up as

a burnt offering in the place of his son. And Abraham named that place The LORD Will Provide. Then the angel of the LORD called to Abraham a second time from heaven, and said, By Myself I have sworn, declares the LORD, because you have done this thing and have not withheld your son, your only son, indeed I will greatly bless you, and I will greatly multiply your seed as the stars of the heavens and as the sand, which is on the seashore; and your seed shall possess the gate of their enemies. And in your seed, all the nations of the earth shall be blessed, because you have obeyed My voice" (Genesis 22: 1 - 18, NASB). Abraham was faithful to God, and he passed the test put before him by God even though he was not sure what the outcome would be. His trust and faith in God must have come from what the Lord had done for him in the past. Abraham knew that God would not fail him and he responded in faith, although he did not know what would happen, however, he believed that God who gave him the son in his old age would neither abandon him nor left him alone. For Abraham not knowing how all will end must be very traumatic to him inwardly. He must have been feeling the pain with the thought that he was on his way to sacrifice his beloved son, the son of his old age. More traumatic to him was the fact that he could not declare to his son that he was on his way to sacrifice him. Having his son carrying the wood to burn him after being killed by his father must be gut ranching for Abraham. However, he continued with the process of following God's command regardless of how emotionally draining the process was for him. Isaac was very obedient to his father and trusted his father in response to his question about everything being ready for the sacrifice except for the absence of the sacrificial animal. Even if he believed his father that the animal would somehow appear, he realized that he was the animal to be sacrificed when his father tied him up. Isaac surrendered to the will of his father without any resistance even when he realized that it might result in the loss of his life. It must be very difficult for both to look at each other's faces when he was lying on the altar wood. Abraham's arm must have felt so heavy when he raised it up to slaughter is only son. However, the Lord came to the rescue at the right time and stopped Abraham from slaughtering his only son. At this point Abraham and Isaac must have been sweating profusely for the fact that none of them wanted what was about to happen to be so. God stopped Abraham and saved the life of Isaac and instead provided an alternative. God was so pleased with Abraham and blessed him and his offspring to come. As a result of Abraham's faithful response to the Lord, God reciprocated His love to Abraham and blessed him with His steadfast love which never ceases, and that unceasing love did not end with Abraham, but continues through his lineage and to the entire world. On several occasions in which the Israelites were disobedient, rebellious, and doubted the power of God, He spared their lives because of the commitment to His promise to Abraham. The remembrance of His steadfast love did not fail or cease to the lineage of Abraham and to the world. Remember that the steadfast love of the Lord never ceases.

"The steadfast love of the Lord never ceases.
His mercies never come to an end.
They are new every morning, new every morning,
Great is Your faithfulness, O Lord,
Great is Your faithfulness"

(The Celebration Hymnal, Songs and Hymns for Worship, #576, 1997).

The blessings Abraham received from God because of his faithful response to God has become continuous blessings to the entire human race through Jesus Christ who came through the linage of Abraham to save the world of their sins and His love will never cease. What is God asking you to give to Him? Are you ready to give a little to God who has given you so much? Are you ready to give Him your life because He is the one Who first gave it to you and Who lost His life to save yours? Are you ready to give Him of your money, time, and/or talent because He is the One Who first gave them to you? Whatever you have or whomever you have become all came from God to you. Whatever God is asking, give it to Him, hilariously. It is important to believe that and remember that God will never forget the good you have done. "For God is not unjust so as to forget your work and the love which you have shown toward His name, by having served and by still serving the saints" (Hebrews 6: 10, NASB).

Isaac and Rebecca

It is expedient that the father and the mother agree on how to raise their children, especially, when a couple has more than one child. Although, children are born of the same parents they might be different in personalities one from the other. Therefore, it is important for parents not to show favoritism to one or the other. Since children are different from each other, parents should be able to treat each child according to each child's Personality. However, parents should avoid showing favoritism to one child over the other. Parents are not helping the children as a family unit if the parents play favoritism. How should the parent respond when the personality of certain children is challenging? The better response for Isaac and Rebecca in managing their family dynamic should have been for them to come into an agreement on a better way to manage their children. There should have been a discussion between Isaac and Rebecca after the initial incident of Esau giving away his birthright for the sake of food. Isaac and Rebecca should have questioned Esau for giving away his birthright for the sake of food when he was hungry and find out the reason his brother, Jacob, did not give him something to eat without requesting for compensation. However, they did not intervene to correct the bad relationship between Esau and Abel, but instead they picked favorites. Since there was no discussion and awareness for a better way to manage their children there was a division in the family with the parents taking sides and showing favoritism. In the Jewish custom the father was to bless the older son at the father's old age before the father's death. Isaac at his old age had poor eyesight and was reliant on his senses of smell and feelings. Isaac was ready to bless Esau, but, Jacob, with the assistance of his mother - Rebecca, deceived Isaac, his father, and Jacob received the blessing meant for his older brother - Esau. When Esau realized that Jacob had defrauded him of his blessings, he was determined, in response, to kill Jacob. In order to save his life Jacob escaped to his mother's brother (his uncle) in another land. The responses of Isaac and Rebecca to the differences in the personality of their sons created hardships for their family. Parents should be sensitive to the feelings of their children, especially, for those parents with three children. There is a phenomenon called 'middle child syndrome' whereby the middle child feels that he/she is not getting enough attention as the first and the last child.

Laban and Jacob

Jacob, the favorite son of Rebecca fled to his mother's brother in another land with the assistance of his mother. While Jacob was with his uncle, he fell in love with the younger of his two nieces. He made this known to his uncle who demanded that Jacob needed to serve him for seven years as the dowry to marry his daughter. It is wise for the people in a contract to be clear of the terms of the contract. Laban and Jacob were not on the 'same page' when it came to the agreement being made to marry Laban's daughter. They did not make a distinction between the two sisters to determine which one Jacob was in love with and who he was willing to marry. Since there was no clear understanding of their contract it created a tough situation at the end of the seven-year service contract. Laban and Jacob were working on assumption of the intention of the other. When in a contract assumption is the wrong means of getting a dependable and banding agreement. Assumption is supposition, presupposition, presumption, premise, belief, speculation, and or guestimate. Those listed definitions above are not exhaustive. Assumptions are dangerous in fostering relationships, in fact, the root cause of troubles in relationships are assumptions as evident in the agreement between Jacob and his uncle with regards to the marriage of his daughters. Jacob's intention was to marry Rachel, but since it was not customary for the younger to be married before the older so Jacob was made to marry Leah, the older of his nieces. Jacob then agreed to work for another seven years to marry his niece with whom he was in love. Jacob could have responded in anger that he was deceived by his uncle, but he accepted the consequence of an unclear verbal contact in order to marry his beloved niece. If Jacob had responded in a confrontational manner with his uncle, he would have lost the ability to stay with his uncle long enough to marry his favorite niece. He would not have only lost the ability to stay with his uncle, but he would have been driven away prematurely.

Therefore, Jacob's measured response bought him time to marry Rachel and to improve his financial wellbeing.

God blessed Jacob for his responses to Laban and Jacob increased in wealth to the point that the servants of Laban despised Jacob. The relationship between Laban and Jacob grew worse to the point that Laban accused Jacob of theft. The situation got worse to the point that Jacob had to notify Leah and Rachel of the worsening relationship between him and their father.

When Laban realized that Jacob had left with his family, with his servants, with his flock and with his two daughters he was angry, especially, when he realized that the family idols were missing. Laban, in fury pursued and went after Jacob. However, the Lord intervened and warned Laban not to speak a word to Jacob whether good or bad but to go easy with him (Genesis 31: 22 - 24, NASB. After Laban caught up with Jacob, he expressed his unhappiness with the manner Jacob left. He wished that Jacob had informed him so he could have sent them all away joyfully. He expressed to Jacob that his family idols were missing. Jacob allowed him to look through his belongings and the belongings of his wives and servants, but Laban did not find the household gods (Genesis 31: 25 - 35, NASB).

At that point Jacob made his unhappiness with the treatments he received from Laban known. He expressed to Laban how Laban did not appreciate all he had done for him for twenty years. In resolving their unhappiness one with the other their responses were to let the other know how he felt with the dynamics of their relationship for about twenty years (Genesis 31: 36 - 42, NASB). In order to resolve their differences, they each let the other know his feelings. They were both opened to each other about their feelings. Their response in openness to each made the resolution of the issues between them easier to get a resolution. It was after this was done that; they were able to resolve their differences. They then came to an agreement/ covenant between them. They collected stones and made a pillar and a heap. They were no longer upset with each other, they ate, and their families stayed together throughout the night. They then made a covenant for Laban never to cross over to the side of Jacob and for Jacob never to cross over the heap and the pillar of stones to Laban's side to wage war. (Genesis 31: 43 - 54, NASB). Their relationships were renewed. Before Laban left the next day, he kissed his daughters and his grandchildren. It was a joyous ending because of their responses to a relationship which had grown worse. The relationship of Laban and Jacob which was getting worse was revived because of their responses to each other. Their responses to each other made the difference.

Jacob Met Esau

Jacob remembered what he had done to his older brother, how he ripped him off his birthright instead of giving him something to eat as a brother. He also remembered how he defrauded him of the blessings their father intended to give to Esau. Jacob remembered that he ran away from home to avoid the wrath of his brother, Esau. If it were possible for Jacob not to return home he would have chosen not to do so, however, that option was not visible. Since he must go home, and he had not had any opportunity to evaluate the demeanor of his brother. He was afraid of what could happen, especially, because he fled home based on the information that his brother was planning to kill him. As he was contemplating what to do about his predicament God assured him not to be afraid and that He would be with him and He told him to return home to his native land. Although God assured Jacob of his safety, he was still afraid of his brother, Esau. In response to his fear, Jacob devised some arrangements to protect his family in case Esau was still angry with him. Here are the steps Jacob took:

First, Jacob sent messengers to Esau to evaluate his mood. In the message he sent to Esau instead of addressing Esau as his brother he addressed him as his Lord, and he addressed himself as Esau's servant - this must be a way to apiece his brother. The messengers delivered Jacobs's message to Esau who was so happy to hear from Jacob that he decided to meet and honor his brother on the way with an entourage of four hundred men. When Jacob heard from his messengers that Esau was coming to meet him with four hundred men his spirit sank in him and he was filled with great fear and distress for himself, for his family, and for his servants. He then thought of what he could do to appease Esau (Genesis 32: 3 - 6, NASB).

Second, Jacob divided the people in his company into two groups, and he divided the animals which were with him into two groups, as well. Jacob's thinking was that if Esau attacked and destroyed one group the other group might escape and survive. (Genesis 32: 7 - 8, NASB).

Third, Jacob prayed and reminded God of God's promise to him to be with him and make him prosper and multiply him. However, he did not stop with his petition to God, but he was still planning on how to appease his brother. In order to appease his brother, he decided to prepare a gift for him. The gift he selected for his brother included two hundred female goats and twenty male goats, two hundred ewes and twenty male rams, thirty female camels with their young, forty cows and ten bulls, and twenty female donkeys and ten male donkeys. He put his servants in charge of each group of animals with some gaps between them. Jacob instructed the leader of each group on what to tell Esau when he met them and asked whose the animals were. They were to tell Esau that those animals were the gift meant for Esau from Jacob, his servant who is coming behind them. (Genesis 32: 9 - 12, NASB)

When Jacob saw Esau coming with his entourage of four hundred men from a far distance, he assigned the children to their mothers. Jacob then went ahead of the women and their children to meet Esau. Jacob responded with humbleness as he approached Esau by bowing down seven times to the ground for Esau. Esau's response was that of elation for seeing Jacob, his brother, who has been gone for a long time, he embraced Jacob, threw his hands around his neck, and kissed him. Esau inquired of the people with Jacob and Jacob told him that they were his family. Esau was also curious about the animals which were in groups and Jacob responded that they were gifts for his Lord, Esau. Esau was blessed with material possession of his own and he did not feel that he needed any gift from his brother. Esau was hesitant to take the gifts, but Jacob persuaded Esau and he took the gifts. Esau responded by taking the gifts not because he needed them, but to allay the fears of Jacob that Esau had not forgiven him. Their meeting turned out not to be as bad as Jacob envisioned because the responses of both were positive (Genesis 33: 1- 16 - NASB). Esau and Jacob maintained a good relationship, thereafter, as evident by both meeting together again to bury their father, Isaac (Genesis 35: 29 - NASB).

Response of Joseph's Brothers

Joseph was the favorite son of his father possibly because he was the son of Jacob's old age or/and because Joseph was the first son of his favorite wife, Rachel. Jacob's love for Joseph was so evident to his brothers that they hated him so much. From his young age he had been going to take care of the flock in the field with his brothers, but he had reported some things to their father which his brothers had done in the field which were not complimentary of them before their father. Jacob showed so much favoritism to Joseph that he bought him a coat of many colors. Joseph made the situational relationship worse with his brothers when he had his first dream which instead of keeping it to himself he declared it to his brothers indicating that they would bow down for him. In his second dream which he did not keep as a secret, as well, he expressed openly to his brothers and to his parents that they were all bowing down to him in his dream. The love his father displayed openly and the two dreams Joseph declared did not help the matter, but made his brothers hate him the more. They were looking for an opportunity to corner him when their parents were not looking to show him who was boss. Such opportunity came when his father sent him to go and check on the welfare of his brothers in the field. When his brothers saw him from a distance away with his flashy garment, they saw the opportunity to destroy him to satisfy the pent-up angers they had against him. Before he got to them, they had decided to kill him, however, their oldest brother, Ruben, intervened with a compromise not to kill him but to throw him into a dry pit from where he could not get out without an assistance. Ruben's plan was to, eventually, pull him out when other brothers were not around. Therefore, they stripped him of his garment of many colors and kept it with them. However, when Ruben was busy with the flock his brothers without any consultation with him sold Joseph to a merchant for twenty shekels of silver. They sold him to the Ishmaelites who took him to Egypt. According to the current foreign exchange rate $0.31353073 is equivalent to one shekel of silver, therefore, twenty shekel of silver is equivalent to about $6.27. Although that amount of money imight be considered to be a small amount today, but it might have a bigger purchasing power at the time. The response of Joseph's brothers to him was devoid of mercy. After throwing him into the pit in the desert, most likey, with no water to drink or shade to protect him, they showed no mercy, they felt comfortable enough to sit down and eat their meal while Joseph was suffering in the pit where they threw him. However, the consequence of their sin caught up with them when they had to go to Egypt during the famine when Joseph had become the Lord of the land. (Genesis 37: 1 – 28, NASB). When they had to face Joseph later in life they regreted their actions in the past and their hearts started to condemn them just as it is stated in 1st John, "Behold, if our heart does not condemn us, we have confidence] before God;" (1 John 3: 21, NASB). When Joseph's brothers were in front of him their hearts were condemning them, and they did not have confidence in themselves talk less of having confidence in God. When you have authority over people today be careful because the next time you encounter them, they might be in position of authority over you and the consequences of your previous response to them might rain heavily down on you for good or for bad. For Joseph he refrained from paying his brothers back for the evil they did him, but instead of retaliation he showed them mercy. How will you respond if you were Joseph? Joseph's brother's saw God in him, will others see Jesus in you if you were in the position of Joseph?

Joseph and Potiphar's Wife

"Now Joseph had been taken down to Egypt by Potiphar, an Egyptian officer of Pharaoh, the captain of the bodyguard, who bought him from the Ishmaelite who had taken him down to Egypt. "The LORD was with Joseph, so he became a successful man. And he was in the house of his master, the Egyptian. Now his master saw that the LORD was with him and how the LORD caused all that he did to prosper in his hand. So, Joseph found favor in his sight and became his personal servant; and he made him overseer over his house, and all that he owned he put in his charge" (Genesis 39: 1 - 4, NASB). "So, he left Joseph in charge of everything that he owned; and with him there he did not concern himself with anything except the food which he ate. Now Joseph was handsome in form and appearance. And it came about after these events that his master's wife had her eyes on Joseph, and she said, sleep with me" (Genesis 39: 6 - 7, NASB). Potiphar's wife inviting Joseph, a young man, to sleep with her was the greatest temptation that Joseph had ever faced. However, Joseph feared God and he considered sleeping with his master's wife, even if his master did not know, was a sin not only against his master but a sin against God. He responded to Potiphar's wife with an unequivocal NO. He explained to Potiphar's wife of how much trust Potiphar had in him. Joseph considered sleeping with his master's wife a betrayal of his master's trust, therefore, he refused to fall into such a temptation. He explained further to Potiphar's wife that her husband entrusted everything in his house into his care, except for her. Joseph explained rationally to Potiphar's wife, but she did not accept Joseph's explanations. She was too infatuated with Joseph that she lost her moral compass. She was insistent on having Joseph sleep with her at every opportunity she had for over an extended period. On one occasion, Potiphar's wife cornered Joseph in an attempt to seduce/entice/force Joseph to sleep with her. Joseph rejected the temporal satisfaction of the moment and instead he obeyed God and followed His direction. God gave Joseph wisdom in his responses as he managed to escape and ran outside to avoid being inside the same house alone with Potiphar's wife. Potiphar's wife was very frustrated and she managed to seize Joseph's garment as he escaped. In retaliation against Joseph, she fabricated a story to her husband and using Joseph's garment as a convincing evidence she reported to Potiphar that the Hebrew slave he brought into their household attempted to rape her. Concerning such a temptation, it could be difficult for a young man such as Joseph to resist. However, Joseph was able to refrain from doing what the flesh would want him to do through God who gave him strength. "I can do all things through Him who strengthens me" (Philippians 4: 13, NASB). Joseph submitted himself and his will to God and God gave him the strength in his response to resist the temptation and not to sin against God. Although Joseph did not commit any sin either against Potiphar or against God, he was rewarded with a prison term. Although Joseph's response to Potiphar's wife landed him in prison God rewarded him in the future, for his faithfulness. Having the right response, at times, could get one into trouble, but God is faithful, and He always comes to the rescue of the innocent.

Joseph in Prison

"So, Joseph's master took him and put him into prison, the same place where the king's prisoners were confined; and he was there in the prison" (Genesis 39: 20, NASB). Pharaoh imprisoned his chief cupbearer and the chief baker in the same prison at the same time as Joseph. "But the LORD was with Joseph and extended kindness to him and gave him favor in the sight of the warden of the prison. And the warden of the prison put Joseph in charge of all the prisoners who were in the prison; so that whatever was done there, he was responsible for it. The warden of the prison did not supervise anything under Joseph's authority, because the LORD was with him; and, the LORD made whatever he did prosper" (Genesis 39: 21 - 23, NASB) . Then the cupbearer and the baker each had different dream on the same night, but the meaning of each one's dream was different. As the overseer of both prisoners Joseph was sensitive to their countenance. He noted that they were sad, and he inquired of them the reason for their sadness. The chief cupbearer told Joseph his dream and Joseph interpreted the dream favorably for him. Then Joseph implored him to remember him after he had been restored to his original position by Pharaoh. The chief baker also told Joseph his dream, but unfortunately the meaning of his dream was tragic. The meaning of the chief baker's dream was that Pharaoh would execute him in three days. God was with Joseph, and He continued to bless him and 'everything was falling into place' positively for him because of his faithfulness, and responses in accordance to the will of God. In a little while after Pharaoh had restored the chief cupbearer into his position Pharaoh had a dream which bordered him and depressed him. "Now in the morning his spirit was troubled, so he sent messengers and called for all the soothsayer priests of Egypt, and all its wise men. And Pharaoh told them his dreams, but there was no one who could interpret them for Pharaoh" (Genesis 41: 8, NASB). Suddenly, after no one in Egypt could interpret Pharaoh's dream, the chief cupbearer remembered and related the story of how a Hebrew young man interpreted the dreams for both, the chief baker and him. The chief cupbearer made plain, based on his own personal experience that everything happened as Joseph said in his interpretations of their dreams. Pharaoh was very curious, and he brought Joseph out of prison in a hurry to give him a chance at interpreting his dream. " Pharaoh said to Joseph, I have had a dream, but no one can interpret it; and I have heard it said about you, that when you hear a dream, you can interpret it. Joseph then answered Pharaoh, saying; It has nothing to do with me; God will give Pharaoh an answer for his own good." (Genesis 41: 14 - 16, NASB). Whenever opportunities presented themselves Joseph's response had always been to give praise to God and to give credit to God instead of soaking in the credit for himself. This was evident in his response to Pharaoh also in this occasion. Pharaoh then recounted his dreams to Joseph. Upon hearing Pharaoh's dreams, Joseph told Pharaoh that the dreams were series of manifestations from God of what would happen soon in the land of Egypt. According to Joseph's interpretation, there would be abundance of food during the first seven years to be followed immediately by another seven years of famine when food would be scarce in the land of Egypt. Joseph did not stop with interpreting the king's dream, but God inclined Joseph to make suggestions to the king on how to manage the first seven years of plenty and the next seven years of famine. Here were the suggestions which Joseph gave to the king "So now let Pharaoh look for a man discerning and wise and appoint him over the land of Egypt. Let Pharaoh take action to appoint overseers in charge of the land and let him take a fifth of the produce of the land of Egypt as a tax in the seven years of abundance. Then have them collect all the food of these good years that are coming and store up the grain for food in the cities under Pharaoh's authority and have them guard it. Let the food be used as a reserve for the land for the seven years of famine which will occur in the land of Egypt, so that the land will not perish during the famine." (Genesis 41: 33 - 36, NASB). Joseph's wise pieces of advice to the king was to be prepared for the fulfilment of God's manifestation of what would happen soon in Egypt. Joseph suggested that Pharaoh needed to put someone

37

of good repute in position to manage the situation to come. Joseph showed kindness and truth in his dealings with Potiphar while he was in Potiphar's household and even in dealing with Potiphar's wife. While in jail Joseph showed kindness to the chief cupbearer and to the chief baker. In all of Joseph's dealings with everyone who was in contact with him he displayed kindness and truth, although things appeared to go worse for him at every turn, he was continually kind and truthful to all. "Do not let kindness and truth leave you; Bind them around your neck, write them on the tablet of your heart. So, you will find favor and good reputation in the sight of God and man. Trust in the LORD with all your heart and do not lean on your own understanding. In all your ways acknowledge Him and He will make your paths straight (Proverbs 3: 5 - 6, NASB). As a result of Joseph's kindness and truthfulness, he continued to receive favor from God and from humans. In his responses to every situation Joseph acknowledged God and gave credit to God for anything which he was able to do at any time. The Lord was pleased with Joseph and He made Joseph's path straight. God gave Joseph favor before Pharaoh and all his servants, and they accepted his proposals. The fact of Joseph's wisdom and faithful dealings with others became known to Pharaoh. Then Pharaoh said to his servants, "Can we find a man like this, in whom there is a divine spirit?" (Genesis 41: 37, NASB). Pondering over the qualifications (discerning and wise?) of who Pharaoh should appoint as overseer in Egypt to conduct Joseph suggested actions, the king concluded that there was no such person in his kingdom.to be in charge. "So, Pharaoh said to Joseph, since God has informed you of all this, there is no one as discerning and wise as you are. You shall be in charge (an overseer) of my house and all my people shall be obedient to you; only regarding the throne will I be greater than you. Pharaoh also said to Joseph, See, I have placed you over all the land of Egypt. Then Pharaoh took off his signet ring from his hand and put it on Joseph's hand, and clothed him in garments of fine linen, and put the gold necklace around his neck. And he had him ride in his second chariot; and they proclaimed ahead of him, Bow the knee! And he placed him over all the land of Egypt. Moreover, Pharaoh said to Joseph, Though I am Pharaoh, yet without your permission no one shall raise his hand or foot in all the land of Egypt" (Genesis 41: 39 - 45, NASB). The Lord was gracious unto Joseph and God elevated him as the second in command in Egypt. No one else besides the king had a higher position than Joseph in Egypt. As the chosen overseer in Egypt, Joseph conducted all the proposals which he prescribed to Pharaoh. Under Joseph's leadership the Egyptians stored food during the first seven years of plenty to be consumed during next seven years of famine. They even had so much food stored than they could consume and people from other regions/nations were travelling to Egypt to buy food. Joseph continued to have favor before God and humans because of his faithful responses to God and everything in his care prospered. Joseph went from prison in Egypt to the palace in Egypt all because of his positive responses to God.

Joseph Response to his Brothers

The famine was so severe in all the surrounding regions of Egypt that people from those regions which were not well prepared for the famine were traveling to Egypt to buy grain. Joseph's brothers who had sold him into slavery some years ago and lied to their father, Jacob, that Joseph was killed by a wild animal also came to Egypt from the land of Canaan. They could not imagine Joseph, their younger brother who they perceived to have died or remained a slave in Egypt to be in such a high-profile position in a foreign land. They have heard so much about the powerful lord of the land in Egypt who was in charge of the grain distribution/sale in Egypt and as a result there was no way they could have ever thought the lord of the land could have been Joseph. Therefore, they did not recognize Joseph when they were in front of him. Joseph was in such an elevated position in Egypt when they got there. After selling him out they had all forgotten about him, but Joseph never forgot his older brothers, his father, and Benjamin, his younger brother. Although Joseph had recognized his brothers, but in his response and dealings with them he did not reveal himself to them. Joseph accused them of being spies and requested that they be imprisoned for three days. " But they said to him, your servants are twelve brothers in all, the sons of one man in the land of Canaan; and behold, the youngest is with our father today, and one is no longer alive. Yet Joseph said to them, it is as I said to you, you are spies, by this you will be tested: by the life of Pharaoh, you shall not leave this place unless your youngest brother comes here! Send one of you and have him get your brother, while you remain confined, so that your words may be tested, whether there is truth in you. But if not, by the life of Pharaoh, you are certainly spies! So, he put them all together in prison for three days" (Genesis 42: 13 - 17, NASB). After their third day in prison, Joseph had human feelings for them and for the sake and fear of God he decided to release all of them but one. He decided that the rest of them should be allowed to buy grain and take it to the rest of their family in Canaan. In order to release the one being held in prison they had to bring Benjamin, their youngest brother to Egypt on their return journey. Through their interactions with Joseph, they made use of an interpreter because Joseph pretended as if he did not understand their language even though he did understand them perfectly well because that was his language too. Joseph's brothers seeing the difficulties they were going through started discussing among themselves in their language without realizing that Joseph understood them. They were discussing that the hardships they were experiencing must have been as a result of their previous sin against Joseph by seizing him when their father sent him to check on their welfare in the field. Joseph, in distress pleaded to them to have mercy on him, but they did not show him mercy. They threw him into a dry pit from which they later fetched him out and sold him to a traveling merchant. They lied to their father, Jacob that a wild animal killed Joseph. In order to convince their father they killed one of their animals and soaked Joseph's clothes in the blood of the animal and showed the clothes to their father. In their conversation with each other they admitted their guiltiness concerning their prior treatment of Joseph. Reuben interjected and reminded them of his opposition to their treatment of Joseph on which they overruled him. He said, "Did I not tell you, 'Do not sin against the boy'; and you would not listen? Now justice for his blood is required." The saying that justice for Joseph's blood was required was an indication of their thought that Joseph had already died sometimes ago. Upon Joseph hearing their conversations he was overcome by emotions, and he went away from them to weep in secrete. When he returned, he seized Simeon and bound him. Simeon was to function as a collateral until they return with Benjamin. Joseph realized that a lot of time had passed since his brothers left Canaan for Egypt and he was concerned that his brother and his parents might have been close to running out of food, therefore, "Joseph gave orders to fill his brothers' bags with grain and also to return every man's money in his sack, and to give them provisions for the journey." Joseph gave them some 'acts of kindness' by having the money of everyone returned into his sack of grain without them knowing it. It was after they had travelled for a while that one of his brothers discovered that the money he paid for his grain was still in his bag of grain. In surprise, he told the rest of his brothers who thought that it was a trap set to accuse them of stealing grain from Egypt. They were perplexed, afraid, and were not able to discern the intention of the man, the lord of the land of Egypt. Although Joseph was troubled by the confession coming out of their mouths to each other concerning their roles in the treatment of him and how they did not show mercy to him despite his pleading to them for mercy, but he instead displayed mercy to them. He did not pay them evil for evil. His response to them was of kindness and forgiveness. Joseph's brothers returned to Canaan. Upon arriving in Canaan, they told Jacob, their father, about their visit to Egypt and how difficult the situation was for them in Egypt. They reported to Jacob that the lord of the land spoke to them harshly and accused them of being spies. They continued to tell their father of their experiences and how they defended themselves as not being spies, but honest men. In order to prove that they were honest men they told the lord of the land that they were twelve brothers, sons of the same father; one already died, and the youngest was with their father in Canaan. But for the lord of the land to believe that they were honest men and not spies they had to leave one of their brothers with him and take grain for their households and go. He then demanded that we bring our youngest brother on the next trip to Egypt. It was after they had satisfied that condition that he would release, Simeon, their brother who was serving as a collateral for them, and after that they could trade in the land. They told Jacob that for that reason they left Simeon in Egypt with the lord of the land as a prisoner collateral. Upon hearing their story Jacob had a flash back regarding Joseph who he sent to check on their welfare in the field several years back and they declared that an animal killed him. Simeon who also went with them to Egypt was detained and he was not sure what would become of him. Therefore, he was not ready to release Benjamin to them being afraid that similar misfortune could occur to him. And their father, Jacob, said to them, you have deprived me of my sons: Joseph is gone, and Simeon is gone, and now you would take Benjamin; all these things are against me. Then Reuben spoke to his father, saying, you may put my two sons to death if I do not bring him back to you; put him in my care, and I will return him to you. But Jacob said, my son shall not go down with you; for his brother is dead, and he alone is left. If harm should happen to him on the journey you are taking, then you will bring my gray hair down to Sheol" (Genesis 42: 29 - 35, NASB). Joseph's brothers upon hearing the refusal of their father to let Benjamin go with them back to Egypt were perplexed and were not sure how to resolve their predicaments. Everything which their father told them was a reasonable possibility of what could happen to Benjamin on the way to Egypt. Jacob was counting his loss thus far and he was not ready to take a gamble with the only son who was left with him and who was serving as his companion. It was a great dilemma for them because they had to take Benjamin to the lord of Egypt in order for him to release Simeon, but their father refused to let Benjamin go with them. Therefore, in this situation Joseph's brothers found themselves 'between the rock and a hard place.' In their frustration with the situation in which they found themselves, Reuben, the eldest son of Jacob, suggested to Jacob that he could use two of his sons as collaterals for Benjamin and he assured Jacob that he was going to take charge of Benjamin all the way to Egypt and return him from Egypt to Jacob safely. In order to assure Jacob that he meant his promise he told Jacob to kill his two sons if he failed to bring Benjamin back to him safely. The situation got a lot more complicated for them because when they emptied their bags of grain the money allotted for each of them to pay for the grain was returned into their bags. They felt that a trap was set for them in order to accuse them of not only being spies, but also for being thieves. This could not have happened at the worst time for them with the fact that their father was afraid and was, therefore, more reluctant to allow Benjamin to go with them to Egypt (Genesis 42: 36, NASB). As an old man Jacob had experienced personal tragedies, the 'death' of Joseph, the captivity of Simeon in Egypt, the loss of his physical abilities, and most likely the decrease in his health. He had only Benjamin to keep him company and to assist him with activities of daily living. He was holding to the only son at his grip, and he would not let him out of his sight for fear of losing him, his last hope. However, they were running out of the grain they bought from Egypt and there was no choice for them but to go back to Egypt to buy more grain. Although Jacob was concerned about Benjamin going with them, however, there was no choice but to allow him to go to Egypt because if they run out of grain they would all die of hunger. Therefore, Jacob released Benjamin reluctantly to them to accompany them to Egypt. Jacob then devised a plan to appease the lord of the land of Egypt. Jacob decided that they should take some gifts to the lord of Egypt. The gifts were little balsam and a little honey, labdanum resin and myrrh, pistachio nuts and almonds. Jacob told them to return the money which was put into their bags during the first trip to Egypt and to take additional money to buy more grain on the present trip. Jacob then allowed Benjamin to go with them to Egypt. Before they left Jacob prayed for them to have favor before the lord of Egypt. Reuben in his response to the concern of their father took a leadership role by taking the full responsibilities for the safe return of Benjamin. He was very persuasive to his father and to convince his father of the seriousness of his commitment by offering two of his children as collateral for the safe return of Benjamin. The commitment of Reuben allayed some of the fears of Jacob when he eventually allowed Benjamin to go with them. Jacob's response was a reliance on God's protection of all his sons on their journey and in their interactions with the lord of the land who happened to be Joseph (in disguise) who Jacob believed was dead a long time ago. (Genesis 43: 1 - 15, NASB).

Joseph Met Benjamin and his brothers

Joseph's brothers arrived in Egypt with Benjamin their youngest brother. Joseph was notified of their arrival and his reaction was inward happiness, but he did not express it to anyone. Joseph was particularly good at hiding his feelings from his brothers. But he told his house steward to bring the men into his house. This was not the usual practice for Joseph, especially, since the men were in Egypt to buy grain. To the surprise of Joseph's house steward Joseph told him to kill an animal, cook it and have it ready for him and the men to eat together for lunch. The house steward brought the men (Joseph's brothers) into Joseph's house. Joseph's brothers were paranoid and were overcome with fear thinking that Joseph was taking them to his house for some form of punishment for not paying for the grain they bought on their first trip to Egypt. They were afraid and the thought going through their minds was that the officers of the lord of the land would attack them in Joseph's house, taking them as slaves, and seizing their donkeys. (Genesis 43: 16 - 17, NASB), Joseph's brothers applied a strategy which has commonly been used in sports, in the military, and in other human endeavors which is referred to as the strategy of offensive principle of war, that strategy states that the best defense is a good offense. Using this principle, before being accused of theft, they told Joseph's house steward that the first time they came to buy grain their money which was intended to pay for the grain was returned into their sacks. They told him that they realized what had happened after they got back to Canaan and that they were returning the money for their first purchase of grain on their first trip. They wanted to come out in the open to prevent being accused of theft, Therefore. They told the house steward plainly that they had money for their purchase on their present trip and for the purchase they made on their previous trip. (Genesis 43: 18 - 22, NASB). Joseph's brothers' response of first telling Joseph's house steward of what happened on their first trip gave them some comfort in showing that they had good intentions and not evil intentions. The response from Joseph's house steward must have given them some comfort. He said, "Peace be to you, do not be afraid. Your God and the God of your father has given you treasure in your sacks; your money was in my possession." (Genesis 43: 23, NASB). Joseph's house steward must have noticed the tremendous fear in their voices and countenance; therefore, he gave them some words of encouragements. Then when Joseph came home, his brothers presented him with the gifts which their father wanted them to give him and they bowed down for him. Joseph responded with interest and concern about their welfare and the welfare of their father. Joseph was very curious to know if their father was still alive. They were happy to tell Joseph that their father was well and alive and in respect to Joseph they bowed down in homage to him again. Looking up, Joseph could not believe his eyes when he saw someone else, who he did not see on their first trip, his youngest brother, of the same mother with him. Joseph wanted to be sure his eyes were not deceiving him and that he was seeing clearly, therefore, he asked his brothers, "Is this your youngest brother, of whom you spoke to me?" The last time Joseph saw Benjamin must have been when he was very young and this time when he saw him again, he was a grown-up man and probably he could not recognize him any longer since his physical appearance must have changed; by then. Benjamin might have grown some beards which he did not have as a lad when Joseph last saw him. Then Joseph said, "May God be gracious to you, my son." Joseph could hardly complete his statement when he was overtaken by emotion, and he had to go out from them to weep in secret. He washed his face before returning to them so that they would not know that he went out to weep because he was not ready to disclose who he was to them. After he returned, he ate the meal and drank together with them. They were full of amazement of what was happening to them in the house of the lord of the land of Egypt. (Genesis 43: 26 - 34, NASB). Joseph was weeping because of the lost time with his brothers and with his parents. He was weeping because of the lack of mercy shown to him by his brothers. Joseph was weeping because he could not spend time with his father. Joseph was also weeping because of how God had been with him throughout his voyages and had blessed him to be next in power to Pharaoh in a foreign land. Joseph saw all the disappointments he had received all along as blessings in disguise. Joseph felt that all that had happened to him was based on the purpose for his life which was driven by God. Every time the situation with Joseph appeared to be turning for the worst, it was a propellant from God to get him to a better situation. The situation with Joseph's life from when his brothers threw him into a pit from where he could never climb out by himself to the time they fetched him out and sold him to a travelling merchant who sold him to Potiphar was directed by God. Then from Potiphar's house he ended up in prison and from there he became the second in power to Pharaoh in Egypt. Joseph's life was a fulfilment of God's purpose for his life. The situation in Joseph's family, especially, the relationship with his brothers was a 'mess' but Joseph turned it into a 'message' of love for his brothers and to his family through the leading of God. Under the instruction of Joseph, the steward of his house filled the men's sacks with food as much as they could carry, and he returned each man's money into the opening of his sack. In addition to putting the money of the youngest man in his sack, the steward of Joseph's house put Joseph's silver cup in his sack according to the instructions from Joseph. Joseph's brothers left on their way back to Canaan for about a distance away from the city when Joseph commanded his steward to hurry and pursue them. Upon catching up with them Joseph instructed the steward to accuse them of theft and to say to them, "Why have you repaid evil for good? Is this not that from which my lord drinks, and which he indeed uses for divination? You have done wrong in doing this!" (Genesis 44: 4 – 5, NASB). When the steward of Joseph's house caught up with them, he accused them of theft and of being ungrateful for the kindness shown them by Joseph, but instead stole his silver cup. Joseph's brothers in proving their innocence recounted how they brought back from Canaan the money which was left in their sacks on their first trip to Egypt. They felt that they were being wrongly accused of theft and they were sure that none of them stole Joseph's silver cup because they did not have access to it in any form. They were so sure in their conviction that they prematurely responded; "With whomever of your servants it is found, he shall die, and we also shall be my lord's slaves." Joseph's steward even suggested a milder punishment for the one with whom the cup was found, instead of killing him he would become a slave and instead of the rest of them becoming slaves they would be free. Upon a thorough searching of all men from Reuben to Benjamin, Joseph's silver cup was found in Benjamin's sack. Their quick response became an immense trouble for them, they tore their clothes in grief, and they returned to the city (Genesis 44: 1 - 13, NASB). Reuben remembered the words of his father before he allowed Benjamin to go with them, he could remember his vow to his father that he took all responsibilities for the safety of Benjamín. The voice of his father could be ringing in his ears saying, if you do not bring Benjamin back to me you will send my soul to Sheol. He must also be thinking about his two sons who he used as collateral/surety that he would bring back Benjamin to Jacob in Canaan and if he should fail to bring him back that his two sons should be killed. As they were going back to the lord of the land's house all those thoughts must have been going through his mind. He could also be thinking that they should not have given such a hasty response that whoever was found with the cup should be killed. His thought could be wondering if Benjamin was going to be put to death by the lord of the land. Reuben was out of words when they got back to Joseph's house, in fact, none of them had words to express their feelings about what happened and how they felt, but all they could do was to fall to the ground before Joseph as an appeal for mercy. Joseph's response appeared as an indication that he was disappointed with how they rewarded him for his kindness to them. Reuben responded, "What can we say to my lord? What words can we speak? And how can we justify ourselves? God has found out the guilt of your servants; behold, we are my lord's slaves, both we and the one in whose] possession the cup has been found" (Genesis 44: 14 - 16, NASB). However, Joseph refused to take them all as captives for the sin of one of them, but instead he told them the one who stole his silver cup deserved to become his slave and others could go back in peace to their father in Canaan.

Then Judah, respectively, approached Joseph and responded to him with humility and recounted the issue of them being accused as spies on their first trip to Egypt. He reminded Joseph that they brought Benjamin on their second trip because Joseph insisted that unless they bring him, he would not welcome them. Reuben told Joseph that their old father was not willing to let Benjamin out of his sight, but he realized that unless Benjamin accompanied them, they would not be able to buy grain in Egypt and Simeon would not be released to them. Therefore, he (Reuben) had guaranteed the safe return of Benjamin, therefore, his father reluctantly allowed him to go with them. He emphasized that if he should return to their father without Benjamin, their father would die in sorrow in his old age. Reuben in his response volunteered himself to become the slave of Joseph in place of Benjamin so his brothers could take Benjamin back to their father. Reuben's response seemed to be a great compromise because he was willing to serve the punishment for the supposed sin of Benjamin (Genesis 44: 17 - 33, NASB).

Joseph Revealed Himself to His Brothers

After the response of Reuben everyone in the house was overtaking by emotion. The situation became emotionally draining for all who were present, and they were all experiencing emotional ups and downs, especially, Joseph's brothers because they were not sure how it would all end as they lost any semblance of control over all the upheavals happening around them. Although Joseph had some form of control over the situation he was almost as equally emotionally 'used up' as the rest of his brothers. Although he has been very stoic all along the way dealing with his brothers, but after Reuben's response Joseph was crushed under the weight of his emotions. He lost control of himself and of his emotions in front of everyone present, therefore, he commanded everyone to leave him besides his brothers. After all Egyptians had left him, he revealed himself to his brothers. Joseph wept so loudly that the Egyptians heard his weeping and the news of it travelled to the house of Pharaoh. "And Joseph said to his brothers, "I am Joseph! Is my father still alive?" But his brothers could not answer him, for they were terrified in his presence. Joseph wanted them not to be terrified of him, therefore, he invited them to come closer to him in order to allay their fears. In response to his invitation, they went closer to him. In his discourse to them he declared his name to be Joseph, their brother who they sold to Egypt. Joseph must have noticed the guiltiness in their demeanor as he disclosed himself to them. They must have had some flash backs to when they were not merciful unto him when he begged them to show him mercy, but instead threw him into the pit. Joseph spoke kind words to them and let them know that their selling him to Egypt was the fulfilment of God's plan and not their fault. Joseph told them that God sent him ahead of them to Egypt to preserve life, therefore, they should not feel guilty about their roles in God's plan. "Now do not be grieved or angry with yourselves because you sold me here, for God sent me ahead of you to save lives. For the famine has been in the land these two years, and there are still five years in which there will be neither plowing nor harvesting. So, God sent me ahead of you to ensure for you a remnant on the earth, and to keep you alive by a great deliverance. Now, therefore, it was not you who sent me here, but God; and He has made me a father to Pharaoh and lord of all his household, and ruler over all the land of Egypt" (Genesis 45: 1 - 8, NASB). What a day of rejoicing that was for them to hear the kind words spoken to them by Joseph their brother, the lord of the land, who they treated mercilessly when they had the opportunity to be kind to him several years ago. They must have been surprised that he did not use his power to crush them but was gentle with them. Their surprise was endless when Joseph implored them to go and bring their father and his household to Egypt in a hurry so he could provide and care for them. They must have felt that they were in a trance upon hearing his response. Joseph fell on Benjamin's neck, kissed him and both wept on each other's necks. Genesis 45: 9 - 15, NASB). As Joseph responded to his brothers saying that all that had happened to all of them was going according to God's plan and that was the reason it all ended well. Their tears turned into joy because the hands of the Lord were in it. Joseph's response was congruent with the proclamation of Paul. "And we know that God causes all things to work together for good to those who love God, to those who are called according to His purpose (Romans 8: 28, NASB). This was evident in the fact that Pharaoh volunteered wagons to carry Joseph's brothers and their belongings to Canaan. Pharaoh also gave permission for the family of Joseph to come and reside in Egypt. The favor Joseph's family began to receive from Pharaoh was nothing less than the fulfillment of the plan of God. Therefore, everything was working together for good. "To each of them he gave changes of garments, but to Benjamin he gave three hundred pieces of silver and five changes of garments. And to his father he sent the following: ten male donkeys loaded with the best things of Egypt, ten female donkeys loaded with grain, bread, and sustenance for his father on the journey" (Genesis 45: 22 - 23, NASB). Joseph's brothers departed from Egypt 'happy as a Clown' to tell their father of the favor they had received in Egypt and above all to tell him that Joseph was alive and that he was the lord of the land in Egypt. The 'lord of the land' of whom their father had heard a lot about before, but who he could not imagine was Joseph his son who was supposedly killed by a wild animal several years ago. When they talked about Joseph and the elevated position which he held in Egypt Jacob could not believe them or what his ears were hearing. However, when Jacob saw the wagons in which they returned and all the gifts with which they came back he believed them. Jacob's countenance and demeanor changed from being depressed to that of elation. He was ecstatic that his son Joseph was alive, and he was eager to travel to see him while he (Jacob) was still alive (Genesis 45: 24 - 28, NASB). Therefore, Jacob and his family moved to Joseph in the land of Egypt with their belongings. The meeting of Joseph with his father was a very joyous occasion. Joseph settled his family in a fertile land for them and their livestock. Their father lived a happy life for the rest of his life in the land of Egypt. After Jacob died, they returned his corpse back to Canaan for burial. However, Joseph's brothers were haunted by their treatment of Joseph of the previous years ago, it was engrained in their brains, and they could not 'let go' of their guiltiness despite Joseph's assurance of his forgiveness to them. They felt that Joseph was being merciful unto them only because their father was still alive, therefore, they believed that Joseph would pay them back for their wrong doings against him. "When Joseph's brothers saw that their father was dead, they said, what if Joseph bears a grudge against us and pays us back in full for all the wrong which we did to him! So, they sent a message to Joseph, saying, your father charged before he died, saying, 'Thus you shall say to Joseph, please forgive, I beg you, the transgression of your brothers and their sin, for they did you wrong. And now, please forgive the transgression of the servants of the God of your father. And Joseph wept when they spoke to him. Then his brothers also came and fell down before him and said, "Behold, we are your servants" (Genesis 50: 15 - 18, NASB). Joseph must have been surprised at his brothers resurrecting their offence against him which he had forgiven them. Joseph was probably upset with them for not allowing 'the sleeping dog lie.' However, in his response he reiterated his prior commitment of forgiveness to them, but he added that he was not God that they should be afraid of him. He also promised to take care of them and their families "But Joseph said to them, do not be afraid, for am I in God's place? As for you, you meant evil against me, but God meant it for good in order to bring about this present result, to preserve many people alive. So, therefore, do not be afraid; I will provide for you and your little ones. So he comforted them and spoke kindly to them" (Genesis 50: 19 - 21, NASB). Joseph's kindly responses to his brothers alleviated their fears and they lived happily in the land of Egypt, thereafter.

Egyptians Response to the Israelites

Joseph was the right-hand person to Pharaoh through whose reign the Israelites were treated well and fairly. Unfortunately, the king who knew Joseph died and a new king who took over the reign in Egypt did not know or cared about Joseph or the Israelites. In fact, the new king might have been wondered why the Israelites were getting such attention and good treatments as foreigners in Egypt. He might have been thinking that all those treatments would be changed once he became king. Sure enough, as soon as he became king his response to what he perceived as undeserved benefits the Israelites were receiving became his focus. He became demagoguery, and to get the Egyptians to join him in his hatred of the Israelites he pointed them to the increasing number of the Israelites. In his lies to them he scarred the Egyptians of what could happen if they did not control the growing numbers of the foreigners amidst them. He demagogued the people against the Israelites. He said to them that if war should break out the Israelites might join the Egyptians' enemies to fight them. The new king started a draconian rule against the Israelites. He put slave masters over them and labored them very hard building Pithom and Rameses as store cities for Pharaoh. What pharaoh did not realize was that the power he thought he had could not be compared to the power of God and that his power could not hinder the plan of God. Therefore, the more he oppressed the Israelites the more they increased in number. The Egyptians increased their harsh treatments of the Israelites. Hatred for the Israelites increased throughout Egypt and the Israelites were made to do very difficult jobs which the Egyptians would not attempt to do. In order words, the Israelites became slaves to the Egyptians. The Israelites continued to increase in number despite the harsh unkind treatments they were receiving from the Egyptians. Pharaoh's response to the failure of his gimmicks to decrease the population of the Israelites was to instruct the midwives to kill the male children of the Israelites during childbirth when they were attending to the women. Whenever the situation appeared/appears bleak was/is when God started to work His ways in the situation. God saw the powerlessness and the helplessness of the Israelites against those in power and He came to their rescue. God put His fear in the minds of the midwives and they preserved the lives of the male children of the Israelites. God worked in the hearts of the midwives to carry out His plan to aid the Israelites in their helplessness. Still Pharaoh questioned the midwives as to why they were sparing the lives of the Israelites' male children and the midwives told him that the Israelites women were very quick in delivering their babes before they ever got to them. As a result of the midwives' actions God blessed them with their own families. Pharaoh was so consumed with his hatred of the Israelites that he gave orders to the Egyptians to drown every Israelites' boy in the Nile (Exodus 1: 1 – 22, NASB). It was during this difficult period for the Israelites in Egypt when Moses was born and his mother hid him. Moses ended up in the king's palace where he was raised by Pharaoh's daughter. The heavy burden of the Israelites became too heavy for them, and they prayed to God to rescue them. God was compassionate on the Israelites, and He answered their requests. At this period God prepared Moses for the task ahead of him as the one to lead the Israelites out of their slavery (Exodus 2: 1 – 25, NASB). This feelings by those in power thinking of losing their power is nothing new. As shown with this situation it has occurred before the birth of Jesus. It also continued during His time when those in power or in the majority fear of their loss of power prompted them to take drastic measures to oppress those who they felt were encroaching on their power. Powerful countries oppress less powerful ones and stronger person oppress a less powerful person. Whenever those who are used to being in power feel a decrease in their power, they formulate lies, deceits, change rules in the middle of the game to get upper hands to maintain their power. When Jesus came into the scene, the Scribes and the Pharisees were afraid of losing their power and as a result demagogued the people to rise against Him until they crucified Him. Political parties do the same when they gain power, they change rules and boundaries to favor their candidates and party in order to maintain power. However, just as God was not happy with the Egyptians and Pharaoh then so He is still not pleased when rules or the treatment are changed or modified by the powerful to benefit the powerful. Just as God was not happy with the Scribes and the Pharisees then for their bending of the rules and laws to satisfy their needs and wants, in the same manner God is not happy with those who explore the poor or the less powerful. God never forgets the poor and the powerless and He comes to their rescue in due time. The Bible was emphatic on the golden rule saying, "In everything, therefore, treat people the same way you want them to treat you, for this is the Law and the Prophets" (Matthew 7: 12, NASB). When one group of people treats another group unkindly, they are not following the golden rule since they would not want to be treated unkindly. The Egyptians under the leadership of Pharaoh treated the Israelites like they did not want to be treated. Their response to God led to their demise in the Red Sea which was their end. Therefore, the response of Pharaoh and the Egyptians and their end should be a lesson to those who oppress others because they have power over them today.

Moses Response to God

God was sympathetic to the plight of the Israelites in Egypt, and He was determined to rescue them from their sufferings. God needed a messenger to conduct His wish, therefore, God chose Moses. When God called Moses to lead the Israelites out of bondage in the land of Egypt Moses' responses were to give all sorts of excuses for why he was not the right person to do the job. The first assignment God gave Moses was to tell Pharaoh to free the Israelites to go. Moses' first response was to say that he was not fit to carry God's message to Pharaoh. God assured him that He will be with him (Exodus 3: 10 - 12, NASB). In Moses' excuse he responded to God with another issue which God had not even delegated him to do by directing his attention to how the Israelites would receive his message. In his second excuse, he said, what if they asked me for God's name? God then told him that he was to tell them that His name is I AM WHO IAM and to emphasize to them that I AM sent him (Exodus 3: 13 - 19, NASB). Moses continued with more excuses because, inwardly, he did not want to do what God was asking him to do. Moses then said, in his third excuse, what if they neither listen to him nor believe that God appeared to him or sent him? The Lord performed two signs, one was turning Moses' staff into a snake and back into the staff and with the other God turned Moses' hand leprous and returned it to normal. In case they did not believe him, the third sign God had for Moses to perform was to turn a small quantity of Nile water into blood (Exodus 4: 1 - 9, NASB). Despite those three signs Moses responded with another excuse. This time his excuse was that he was not eloquent. Moses said that he has always been slow of speech and tongue before and after God had spoken to him. God told Moses that the problem he enumerated was amazingly simple for Him to take care of because He would go ahead of him, and He will teach him what to say in the situation. Upon hearing about the promise of God to support him

Moses realized that all excuses had not worked then he came out plainly with what was in his mind about God's request. He then told God to send someone else. In other words, Moses refused to do what God wanted him to do by telling God to send someone else with the hope that God would leave him alone. If that was his thought, he was very wrong because God became angry with him because of his responses to the message of God. Although God was angry with Moses, He provided a way out for him by suggesting to him that Aaron, his brother could accompany him and be a spokesperson for him. (Exodus 4: 10 - 17, NASB).

Moses and Aaron delivered the Lord's message to Pharaoh to let the Israelites go so they could worship the Lord in the wilderness. Pharaoh's response upon hearing the request was anger. He felt that the only reason the Israelites had time to plan to leave was because they were not worked hard enough. He commanded the slave drivers to stop providing the Israelites with the raw materials they needed to do their work but instead to have the Israelites fetch the raw materials they needed and to still produce the same number of products as when the raw materials were being provided for them. Pharaoh doubled the Israelites workload. Moses followed the Lord directives and turned his staff into a snake; however, the Egyptian magicians replicated the same sign, but the snake of Moses swallowed the snake of the magicians. As a result of the response of Pharaoh all the Egyptians suffered, when under the direction of God all the bodies of water turned bloody starting with the Nile River. The fish died and the water stunk making the Egyptian waters in Egypt non-drinkable (Exodus 7: 14 - 24, NASB). The Egyptians had to dig along the Nile River before they could get water to drink. The Lord did not relent in His request through Moses and Aaron to tell Pharaoh to let the Israelites go. Instead of listening to the word of God through Moses and Aaron Pharaoh refused to let the Israelites go. As a result of Pharaoh's response God sent a plague of frogs which tormented all Egyptians. No one in Egypt, including Pharaoh escaped the torment of the frogs in all activities of their lives outside and inside their homes including the palace. Pharaoh made a false promise that he would let the Israelites leave the next day, but he did not keep his promise (Exodus 8: 1 - 15, NASB). Because Pharaoh's response was of a deceit; another plague invaded his land and troubled his people. This time it was the plague of gnats. The dust everywhere in Egypt turned into gnats and they settled on all humans and animals which

was another consequence to Pharaoh's response to God's request to let the Israelites go (Exodus 8: 16 - 19, MASB).

God did not relent on His request of Pharaoh to let the Israelites go, but instead for Pharaoh to obey the request of the Lord his response was of defiance and rejection of the Lord's request. Due to Pharaoh's response to God the life of Pharaoh and of the Egyptians were made uncomfortable through the plague of swarms of flies. The swarms of flies landed on Pharaoh, his officials, and on all the Egyptians. The swarm of flies not only settled on all human beings in Egypt, but they invaded their homes, as well. As a result of Pharaoh's responses to God all the Egyptians suffered. However, Pharaoh made another promise that he would let the Israelites go as a ploy to get relief from the invading flies, but he did not intend to keep his promise to let the Israelites go. He reneged on his promise again and as a result another plague invested his land (Exodus 8: 20 - 32, NASB). Pharaoh thought that he could deceive God with impunity and as a result he was responding to God's request with disobedience and insincerity of heart. Each disobedience and insincere response was met with God's punishment. God continued His request and Pharaoh continued to respond in defiance to the Lord. His rebellious responses to the Lord brought harsh repercussions not only to him and his people, but also to their animals. The plague fell on the Egyptian horses, donkeys, camels, cattle, sheep, and goats which killed them. Even with the plague on the Egyptian livestock Pharaoh did not succumb to the will of the Lord to let the Israelites go, but his response was hard heartedness (Exodus 9: 1 - 7, NASB). Since Pharaoh did not bend his will to the purpose of God his response was contrary to God's request and for such response he and his people faced physical plague of boils. All Egyptians and their animals were inflicted with the plague of boils (Exodus 9: 8 - 12, NASB). Pharaoh continued to flex his muscles against the will of God and his response to God was of disrespect and refusal to yield to His will. This response provoked the Lord with a response of inflicting the land of Egypt with hail. All animals and people who did not get under the protection of God in the shelter died in the hail (Exodus 9: 13 - 35, NASB).

The Plagues in Egypt

God did not give up on getting Pharaoh to reconsider his response of refusal to let the Israelites go. God continued to send Moses and Aaron back to Pharaoh requesting that he allow the Israelites to leave Egypt. The more God's request was presented to Pharaoh the more he was determined to continue in his response of refusal. However, Pharaoh was adamant in his response with refusal to submit to the request from God. With each of the plagues before, God made it plain to Pharaoh through Moses and Aaron that He would allow the plague to invade Egypt. God always forewarned Pharaoh of the impending consequences that would follow each of Pharaoh's response even before it happened. However, despite the warning from the Lord Pharaoh was determined not to listen to the messengers of God and not to do as God requested. In this occasion God allowed locust to invade the land of Egypt. All their plants, the plants of Pharaoh, the plants of his officials, as well as the plants of all the Egyptians were consumed by locust. The locust even went into their homes and made life miserable for the Egyptians. When life in Egypt became very unbearable, Pharaoh had a pseudo confession of his sins and promised to let the Israelites go, this also was neither a wholehearted confession nor a promise to keep. After God removed the locusts, Pharaoh continued his hard heartedness and refusal to let the Israelites go. (Exodus 10: 1 - 20, NASB). God then brought darkness on the land of Egypt for three days and the Egyptians could not see each other because of the thickness of the darkness. However, there was light where the Israelites lived. Pharaoh was so angry with Moses and Aaron that he threatened to kill them if they ever came back to him again (Exodus 10: 21 - 29, NASB). When God is determined to do anything, no human force could stop Him. God was determined to rescue the Israelites from the grip of Pharaoh, but Pharaoh responses had been to stall the plan of God. As a result of the obstinate responses of Pharaoh God allowed the death of all the first born of the Egyptians, the male first born of their slaves, and the male first born of their animals while sparing the live of every living thing belonging to the Israelites. All those things happened as the Lord declared the consequences of Pharaoh's responses to the request from the Lord to let the Israelites go. The consequence of sin is not always limited to the sinner, but other people or the nation could be affected, as well. All Egyptians were being punished for the sin of Pharaoh (Exodus 12: 29 - 36, NASB). After God's severe punishments on the Egyptians Pharaoh finally allowed the Israelites to leave Egypt. However, not long after the Israelites had left Egypt the Egyptians missed the services which the Israelites were performing, therefore, they pursued them hoping to capture them and bring them back to Egypt.

But the Lord disguised the Israelites and protected them with a pillar of cloud by day and pillar of fire by night which made it impossible for the Egyptians to visualize them even when they were close to them by day and provided light for the Israelites to see to continue their journey at night, respectively. The Egyptians, Pharaoh, and his army caught up with the Israelites as the Israelites were crossing the Nile River on dry land.

They pursued the Israelites into the dry sea, but as the Israelites completed crossing the sea all the Egyptians, their king, Pharaoh, were swept away and died in the sea. This was the final consequence of Pharaoh's response to God (Exodus 14: 5 - 30, NASB). The

Israelites continued their journey with their families, their animals, their servants, and all their belongings. As they went along, they experienced varieties of obstacles including lack of water, food, and the fierce desert conditions. Then the Israelites complained, " But the whole congregation of the sons of Israel grumbled against Moses and Aaron in the wilderness. The sons of Israel said to them, "If only we had died by the LORD'S hand in the land of Egypt, when we sat by the pots of meat, when we ate bread until we were full; for you have brought us out into this wilderness to kill this entire assembly with hunger!" (Exodus 16: 2 - 3, NASB). The Israelites portrayed human trait in that when humans face hardships or difficulties they perceived the present hardships or difficulties as being worse than they have ever encountered. Humans have tendencies to forget how God had helped them with previous hardships or difficulties. The Israelites forgot all the wonders the Lord performed to get them out of Egypt and the Lord's protection for them in crossing the sea on dry land followed by His destruction of Pharaoh, his army, and his people who were determined to destroy them. They complained against God, Moses, and Aaron and accused them of taking them into the desert to die. When they lacked water and food earlier in their journey the Lord provided. "Then the LORD said to Moses, "Behold, I will rain bread from heaven for you; and the people shall go out and gather a day's portion every day, so that I may test them, whether they will walk in My instruction. On the sixth day, when they prepare what they bring in, it will be twice as much as they gather daily" (Exodus 16: 4 - 5, NASB). However, when they lacked water again, they were upset with Moses and Aaron, and they quarreled with them. The Israelites allowed the difficulties of the moment to control their emotions. It is always exceedingly difficult for a leader to lead a group of ungrateful people. Leading such people could create emotional distress for a leader thus causing the leader to behave in an irrationally unusual manner as it happened to Moses. Moses was terribly upset with the situation and with the ungratefulness of the Israelites, as well as their lack of trust in God. Moses prayed to the Lord and God instructed Moses to speak to the rock and water would flow out of the rock for the people to drink.

However, Moses was so upset with the Israelites that he took his eyes away from the Lord and he followed his emotional feelings in disregard to the instruction from the Lord. Instead of speaking to the rock he struck the rock twice. God became unhappy with Moses for his response, and He prevented Moses from reaching the promised land. "So, Moses took the staff from before the LORD, just as He had commanded him; and Moses and Aaron summoned the assembly in front of the rock. And he said to them, listen now, you rebels; shall we bring water for you out of this rock?

Then Moses raised his hand and struck the rock twice with his staff; and water came out abundantly, and the congregation and their livestock drank. Even when humans refused to follow the direction from God, God could still fulfil His purpose as was in this case, although Moses failed to follow God's direction God still provided water for the Israelites through Moses' fallible action. But the LORD said to Moses and Aaron, since you did not trust in Me, to treat Me as holy in the sight of the sons of Israel, for that reason you shall not bring this assembly into the land which I have given them" (Numbers 20: 9 -12, NASB). Moses' momentary angry response deprived him of the opportunity to reach the promised land for which he had labored in the desert for several years. It is important for humans to keep their eyes on the Lord and not to allow reactions to issues of this world to distract them from following the will of the Lord.

The Golden Calf

"Now when the people saw that Moses delayed to come down from the mountain, the people assembled around Aaron and said to him, Come, make us god who will go before us; for this Moses, the man who brought us up from the land of Egypt—we do not know what happened to him. Aaron said to them, Tear off the gold rings which are in the ears of your wives, your sons, and your daughters, and bring them to me. So, all the people tore off the gold rings which were in their ears and brought them to Aaron. Then he took the gold from their hands and fashioned it with an engraving tool and made it into a cast metal calf; and they said, This is your god, Israel, who brought you up from the land of Egypt. Now when Aaron saw this, he built an altar in front of it; and Aaron made a proclamation and said, tomorrow shall be a feast to the LORD. So the next day they got up early and offered burnt offerings, and brought peace offerings; and the people sat down to eat and to drink, and got up to engage in lewd behavior.

Then the LORD spoke to Moses, Go down at once, for your people, whom you brought up from the land of Egypt, have behaved corruptly. They have quickly turned aside from the way which I commanded them. They have made for themselves a cast metal calf, and have worshiped it and have sacrificed to it and said, This is your god, Israel, who brought you up from the land of Egypt! Then the LORD said to Moses, have seen this people, and behold, they are an obstinate people. So now leave Me alone, that My anger may burn against them and that I may destroy them; and I will make of you a great nation" (Exodus 32: 1 – 10, NASB).

Moses Responded to God in a Plea

Then Moses pleaded with the LORD his God, and said, LORD, why does Your anger burn against Your people whom You have brought out from the land of Egypt with great power and with a mighty hand? Why should the Egyptians talk, saying with evil motives He brought them out, to kill them on the mountains and to destroy them from the face of the earth'? Turn from Your burning anger and relent of doing harm to Your people. Remember Abraham, Isaac, and Israel, Your servants to whom You swore by Yourself, and said to them, 'I will multiply your descendants as the stars of the heavens, and all this land of which I have spoken I will give to your descendants, and they shall inherit it forever.'" So the LORD relented of the harm which He said He would do to His people. (Exodus 32: 11 – 14, NASB). Moses was very disappointed with what the Israelites under the leadership of Aaron had done. They had quickly forgot who their Savior was but replaced the true God with a god made by hands and gave it credit for rescuing them out of Egypt. Although Moses was disappointed with what the Israelites had done, he did not allow his disappointment to be in the way of his plea to God to have mercy on the Israelites and to spare their lives. In Moses' plea to God he made clear that the Egyptians and all the nations around would belittle the power of God and believe that God was not able to complete the mission of saving the Israelites which He started and because of His (God's) inability to complete His mission He destroyed the Israelites. Moses said that such perceived reputation would not look good for the name of God. Therefore, Moses appealed to the Lord to relent His anger. As a result of Moses' reasonable response and intervention God spared the lives of the Israelites.

Moses and Joshua, Puzzled

"Then Moses turned and went down from the mountain with the two tablets of the testimony in his hand, tablets which were written on both sides; they were written on one side and the other. The tablets were God's work, and the writing was God's writing engraved on the tablets. Now when Joshua heard the people as they shouted, he said to Moses, there is a sound of war in the camp. But he said,

It is not the sound of the cry of victory,
Nor is it the sound of the cry of defeat;

But I heard the sound of singing" (Exodus 32: 15 – 18, NASB). Moses and Joshua could not believe the sound coming from the camp where the Israelites, and Aaron, their leader were. They did not know what to make of the noises which appeared to be a mixture of the sound of victory and the sound of defeat. They were puzzled on their way to the camp.

Moses Responded in Anger

"And it came about, as soon as Moses approached the camp, that he saw the calf and the people dancing; and Moses' anger burned, and he threw the tablets from his hands and shattered them to pieces at the foot of the mountain. Then he took the calf which they had made and completely burned it with fire, and ground it to powder, and scattered it over the surface of the water and made the sons of Israel drink it. Then Moses said to Aaron, What did this people do to you, that you have brought such a great sin upon them? And Aaron said, Do not let the anger of my lord burn; you know the people yourself, that they are prone to evil. For they said to me, 'Make a god for us who will go before us; for this Moses, the man who brought us up from the land of Egypt—we do not know what happened to him. So I said to them, 'Whoever has any gold, let them tear it off. Then they gave it to me, and I threw it into the fire, and out came this calf. Now when Moses saw that the people were out of control—for Aaron had let them get out of control to the point of being an object of ridicule among their enemies—Moses then stood at the gate of the camp, and said, Whoever is for the LORD, come to me!" And all the sons of Levi gathered together to him. And he said to them, This is what the LORD, the God of Israel says: 'Every man of you put his sword on his thigh, and go back and forth from gate to gate in the camp, and kill every man his brother, and every man his friend, and every man his neighbor. So the sons of Levi did as Moses instructed and about three thousand men of the people fell that day. Then Moses said, dedicate yourselves today to the LORD—for every man has been against his son and against his brother—in order that He may bestow a blessing upon you today. And on the next day Moses said to the people, You yourselves have committed a great sin; and now I am going up to the LORD; perhaps I can make atonement for your sin. Then Moses returned to the LORD and said, Oh, this people has committed a great sin, and they have made a god of gold for themselves! But now, if You will forgive their sin, very well; but if not, please wipe me out from Your book which You have written! However, the LORD said to Moses, Whoever has sinned against Me, I will wipe him out of My book. But go now, lead the people where I told you. Behold, My angel shall go before you; nevertheless on the day when I will punish them for their sin. Then the LORD struck the people with a plague, because of what they did with the calf which Aaron had made (Exodus 32: 19 – 35, NASB). Aaron was not steadfast in faith in God, therefore, he succumbed to pressure from the Israelites. Aaron had been with Moses from the beginning of the process of God to get the Israelites out of bondage in Egypt. Aaron had gone through the difficulties of dealing with Pharaoh and how God intervened. He had experienced how Moses had handled the Israelites during the journey with their lack of gratefulness to God and how much pressure they had put on Moses. Aaron had also seen how Moses had worked in tandem with God whenever any issue arose. All the issues and difficulties through their journey Aaron saw how Moses consulted with God to arrive at a solution. Aaron, also, had witnessed how the Israelites had responded to God and Moses with every inconvenience and how God had used Moses to handle the Israelites. Through all his experiences of God through Moses Aaron should not have been caught 'flat footed' (unprepared) when the Israelites came up with their troubles. Aaron should have known how to handle them with their complaints and fears. Aaron should have consulted with God just as Moses had done several times in his presence. However, Aaron did not do any of those things which he knew to do, but he instead yielded control over to the Israelites instead of to God. Aaron succumbed to the pressure from the people but instead of being the light to them he brought them darkness. Aaron knew what was right to do but he did what was easy to please the Israelites, he made a golden calf out of the jewelry they were wearing and proclaimed it their god. James declared, " So for one who knows the right thing to do and does not do it, for him it is sin" (James 4: 17, NASB). Through his actions Aaron sinned and led the Israelites to sin and presided over their sin by declaring a day of celebration to worship the golden calf as the god who rescued them from Egypt. It is easy to condemn Aaron if one has never been under the pressure of mob subordinates. However, anyone who has been in a leadership role could attest to the fact that it is difficult to stand for the truth and for doing what is right without fallen victim to pressure. The only way to stand up to the pressure and what is right is by being close to God, by relying, and leaning on Him for direction on every action. Therefore, in condemning Aaron, the reader should pay close attention to the word of Paul in this admonition saying, "Brethren, even if anyone is caught in any trespass, you who are spiritual, restore such a one in a spirit of gentleness; each one looking to yourself, so that you too will not be tempted" (Galatians 6: 1, NASB). Although Moses was not happy with what Aaron did, but he was gentle in his response to him. Moses then tested the loyalty of the Israelites to God by seeking responses from them to show their loyalty or disloyalty to God. Those Israelites who responded with loyalty to God were saved, but those who responded in disloyalty to God were destroyed. In this occasion the responses of the Israelites led to either their staying alive or being dead. Their responses meant life or death.

A Journey of 40 Days took 14,610 Days

God appreciates people's faith and the trust in Him in all aspects of life, in every situation, and in all circumstances even when it appears that there is no way out of the situation. God will provide a way. The truth about God providing a way is brought to life in the lyric of the song by Don Moen;

"God will make a way
Where there seems to be no way
He works in ways we cannot see
He will make a way for me
He will be my guide
Hold me closely to His side
With love and strength for each new day
He will make a way, He will make a way
Oh, God will make a way
Where there seems to be no way
He works in ways we cannot see
He will make a way for me
He will be my guide
Hold me closely to His side
With love and strength for each new day
He will make a way, He will make a way
By a roadway in the wilderness, He'll lead me
Rivers in the desert will I see
Heaven and earth will fade but His Word will remain
And He will do something new today
Oh, God will make a way
Where there seems to be no way
He works in ways we cannot see
He will make a way for me
He will be my guide
Hold me closely to His side

With love and strength for each new day
He will make a way, He will make a way
Who might be here tonight
You may think God has forgotten you
About your situation, but He hasn't
The Bible says that we are inscribe in the palm of His hand
And Heaven and earth may pass away
But His word will remain forever
And He can do exceedingly, abundantly
Above all that we could ever ask or think tonight (amen)
Amen, let's sing it
Oh, God will make a way
Where there seems to be no way
He works in ways we cannot see
He will make a way for me
He will be my guide
Hold me closely to His side
With love and strength for each new day
He will make a way, He will make a way
With love and strength for each new day
He will make a way; He will make a way."

The Israelites experienced the miraculous ways God took them out of bondage in Egypt and how He had protected and provided for them through their treacherous journey in the desert. The protection and the provision of God for all their needs should have been enough to 'cement' their faith in God. All promises and commitments of God to them on their journey were fulfilled in their presence. They had gone through fierce wars along their journey, and they were victorious through their faith and obedience to God. Their experiences of the love God had bestowed on them should have made them trust God when He promised to give the land of Canaan to them and as an inheritance to their generation. But, instead of trusting, they allowed their fears to be in the way of their faith in God. God wanted to give the Israelite a 'taste' of the land in form of the fertility of the soil and the type of the inhabitants of the land. God might have wanted the Israelites to have a glimpse of the land to arouse their interest in wanting to do everything to acquire such a good land and to increase their reliance on Him to help them conquer the land knowing that in their power they were no match to the inhabitants of the land. Therefore, the process of sending twelve spies might have been to give them a sneak preview of the land, a test of their faith, and a check of their reliance on God. If the process was really a test, the Israelites failed it woefully bad. Ten of the spies made the matter worse for the grumblers, the Israelites, when they came back with mis-matched report of the land. One could ask the question, on whose side were the ten spies? The resounding answer to that rhetoric question would be that they were neither on the side of the Israelites for their good nor on the side of God in obedience to Him. Then if they were still not on the side of God, therefore, they must have been on the side of the devil to diminish the Israelites faith in God. So, the ten spies gave a bad report of the promised land to the Israelites. "When Moses sent them to spy out the land of Canaan, he said to them, go up there into the Negev; then go up into the hill country. See what the land is like, and whether the people who live in it are strong or weak, whether they are few or many. And how is the land in which they live, is it good or bad? And how are the cities in which they live, are the people in open camps or in fortifications? And how is the land, is it productive or unproductive? Are there trees in it or not? And show yourselves courageous and get some of the fruit of the land." Now the time was the season of the first ripe grapes" Numbers 13: 17 - 20, NASB). In commissioning the twelve to spy the promised land Moses requested the following information back from them regarding the nature of the land, the strength of the inhabitants, the number of the inhabitants (few or many), nature of the fortification of the cities, and the productivity of the land. The twelve saw the same land but broke into two camps in their report to the Israelites. The division of the twelve was ten against two. Christians must use this incident as a caution not to switch over based on quantity of the people on one side on any issue because the majority being on one side does not mean that the side is doing what is pleasing to God. "And do not be conformed to this world, but be transformed by the renewing of your mind, so that you may prove what the will of God is, that which is good and acceptable and perfect" (Romans 12: 2, NASB). Although the two were outnumbered they refused to conform with the ten spies who they perceived were not doing the will of God. The two spies held tightly to their stand to follow the will of God, stuck to the truth and the perfect will of God was eventually fulfilled for them and for the Israelites. The ten spies were taking the minds of the people away from God while the second group comprising of only two spies was keeping the Israelites in the grace of God. However, the Israelites listened and were persuaded by the majority group with the ten spies. Even though the spies brought back a single bunch of grapes, pomegranates, and figs. "When they returned from spying out the land, at the end of forty days, they went on and came to Moses and Aaron and to all the congregation of the sons of Israel, in the wilderness of Paran at Kadesh; and they brought back word to them and to all the congregation and showed them the fruit of the land. So, they reported to him and said, we came into the land where you sent us, and it certainly does flow with milk and honey,

and this is its fruit. Nevertheless, the people who live in the land are strong, and the cities are fortified and very large. And indeed, we saw the descendants of Anak there! Amalek is living in the land of the Negev, the Hittites, the Jebusites, and the Amorites are living in the hill country, and the Canaanites are living by the sea and by the side of the Jordan. Then Caleb quieted the people before Moses and said, we should by all means go up and take possession of it, for we will certainly prevail over it. But the men who had gone up with him said, we are not able to go up against the people, because they are too strong for us. So, they brought a bad report of the land which they had spied out to the sons of Israel, saying, "The land through which we have gone to spy out is a land that devours its inhabitants; and all the people whom we saw in it are people of great stature. We also saw the Nephilim there (the sons of Anak are part of the Nephilim); and we were like grasshoppers in our own sight, and so we were in their sight. Then all the congregation raised their voices and cried out and the people wept that night. And all the sons of Israel grumbled against Moses and Aaron and the entire congregation said to them, if

only we had died in the land of Egypt! Or even if we had died in this wilderness! So why is the LORD bringing us into this land to fall by the sword? Our wives and our little ones will become plunder! Would it not be better for us to return to Egypt? So, they said to one another, Let's appoint a leader and return to Egypt! Then Moses and Aaron fell on their faces in the presence of all the assembly of the congregation of the sons of Israel. And Joshua the son of Nun and Caleb the son of Jephunneh, of those who had spied out the land, tore their clothes; and they spoke to all the congregation of the sons of Israel, saying, "The land which we passed through to spy out is an exceedingly good land. If the LORD is pleased with us, then He will bring us into this land and give it to us, a land which flows with milk and honey. Only do not rebel against the LORD; and do not fear the people of the land, for they will be our prey. Their protection is gone from them, and the LORD is with us; do not fear them. But all the congregation said to stone them with stones. Then the glory of the LORD appeared in the tent of meeting to all the sons of Israel" (Numbers 13: 23 - 33; 14: 10 NASB).

The ten spies were very pessimistic in their report. They did not tell the whole truth about the land they visited. It will always remain a misery what their motives were as the leaders of their tribes to bring such depressing news about the land they saw. As the leaders of their tribes, they were in positions to encourage their people but instead they discouraged and scared them. At certain point they declared that the land they visited devour its inhabitants, however, if that was true there should have not been any person living in that land. Then they said the inhabitants were giants to whom they appeared like grasshoppers, then, if it was true that the land devours its inhabitants, from where did those giants come? Even if those inhabitants were giants and strong men, they should have known that God was stronger than those giants. The spies took their focus and the focus of the Israelites away from God and focused it on the perceived problems. The ten spies saw issues as obstacles instead of looking at them as challenges which God was ready to solve for them only if they had faith. Attempts by Caleb and Joshua to bring the people back to reality of God's power and mercy failed because the ten spies influenced the mind of the people wrongly. Therefore, the Israelites blamed Moses, Aaron, and God for taking them out of their slavery in Egypt. They felt that their condition of enslavement and torture in Egypt was preferable to their current uncertain situation in the desert. They abandoned God, Moses, and Aaron at the time they needed all most and at one point they intended to stone both Moses and Aaron. They rejected God as their leader, and they wanted a different human leader to lead them back into slavery in Egypt. God was very unhappy with them because in their responses they rejected and minimized the love, providence, and power of God to save them. They provoked God to anger, and He was determined to destroy them all. God was very curious and asked Moses, as if Moses knew. "And the LORD said to Moses, how long will this people be disrespectful to Me? And how long will they not believe in Me, despite all the signs that I have performed in their midst? I will strike them with plague and dispossess them, and I will make you into a nation greater and mightier than they" (Numbers 14: 11-12, NASB). God considered the responses of the Israelites as being disrespectful to Him by limiting His ability and power as if they had never witnessed the miracles He had been performing in their midst. However, Moses was considerate of the reputation of God, and he said to God, when the Egyptians hear that God took them out of Egypt and killed them in the desert because He was not able to carry out His plan to save them. Moses conversed with God that such an action could tarnish the image of God before the pagan worshipers around the region.

"But Moses said to the LORD, Then the Egyptians will hear of it, for by Your strength You brought this people up from their midst and they will tell it to the inhabitants of this land. They have heard that You, LORD, are in the midst of this people, because You, LORD, are seen eye to eye, while Your cloud stands over them; and You go before them in a pillar of cloud by day, and in a pillar of fire by night. Now if You put this people to death all at once, then the nations who have heard of Your fame will say, Since the LORD could not bring this people into the land which He promised them by oath, He slaughtered them in the wilderness.' So now, please, let the power of the Lord be great, just as You have declared, saying, The LORD is slow to anger and abundant in mercy, forgiving wrongdoing and violation of His Law; but He will by no means leave the guilty unpunished, inflicting the punishment of the fathers on the children to the third and the fourth generations. Please, forgive the guilt of this people in accordance with the greatness of Your mercy, just as You also have forgiven this people, from Egypt even until now" (Numbers 14: 13 - 19, NASB).

The journey of Forty Days took 14,610 Days.

Although God relented in His anger to destroy all the Israelites at one time, but instead, He spread out their death over forty years. It took the spies forty days to reach the land of Canaan and as a punishment of their unbelief God made the distance covered in one day take a duration of one year and as a result the journey which took the spies 40 days took the Israelites 40 years to reach the promised land. The promised land was within their reach in 40 days, but because of their unbelief it took them 14,610 days (40 years) instead. "So, the LORD said, I have forgiven them in accordance with your word; however, as I live, all the earth will be filled with the glory of the LORD. Certainly, all the people who have seen My Glory and My signs which I performed in Egypt and in the wilderness yet have put Me to the test these ten times and have not listened to My voice, shall by no means see the land which I swore to their fathers, nor shall any of those who were disrespectful to Me see it. But as for My servant Caleb, because he has had a different spirit and has followed Me fully, I will bring him into the land which he entered, and his descendants shall take possession of it" (Numbers 14: 21 - 24, NASB). The responses of the Israelites brought serious repercussions on them from God. They wandered aimlessly in the wilderness for 14,610 days instead of 40 days. Those who were of age when they left Egypt and who were aware pf God's wonderful works among them did not live to reach the land of Canaan. Their children suffered for the sins of their parents as a collateral inadvertent punishment. All those hardships fell on them because of their responses to the will of God for them. However, the Lord stepped back in His decision to destroy them all at once because of the reasonable responses and intervention of Moses. There are multiple examples in the Bible where God relented in punishing or destroying His people as a result of the intervention of His chosen ones. In those occasions, God stepped back from punishing the people of the world for their sins. However, stepping back by God from punishing the people of the world was not enough to bury their sins, therefore, God in His infinite wisdom decided to step forward by sending Christ to take away the sins of the world once for all. Because God stepped forward in this manner, the sins of the world was laid on Christ for which He received severe punishment up to death for the sins of all in the past, present, and in the future. The question becomes what is the cost to the individuals in the world? The answer to that question is "it is free" because Christ paid it all. If Christ paid it all what should the response to Christ sacrificial giving of Himself be? The response from all human beings should be, believing in the Lord Jesus Christ to be saved. What has your response been to Christ or what will your response be to Him who had sacrificed all for your salvation? Remember that the consequence of your responses to Christ is whether you spend eternity with Him and the father or away from both to be with the devil eternally. Accept Him and all will be well with you in this world and in the world to come.

Falling of the Wall of Jericho

The military strategy which God gave to Joshua did not seem to be a plan that could lead to victory and success, but fraught with high probability for defeat and failure which no military leader will embark on for his troops. It did not appear to be a winning strategy in human thinking, but what appeared to be a bad strategy on its face was a successful God's plan to defeat and conquer Jericho. Military operations, generally, are carried out against the enemy by stealth, without announcement or open actions that could get the enemy ready for a counterattack. Especially, considering the report brought back by the ten of the twelve spies. However, the plan did not make sense with human understanding and plans, God's plan is different from human plans because He could see the beginning and the end of things and events. God could foresee how things would end. Joshua was aware of God's ability to lead successfully, therefore, his response was to do as God had instructed. Joshua responded with his experience of God's mighty power to save. Joshua was obedient to God in his response to Him and he passed God's plan on to the Israelites. God assured Joshua that it was a 'done deal' that he had handed Jericho over to the Israelites and that all that was left was for them to go and conquer Jericho. God was very explicit in giving Joshua His winning formula. God told Joshua, "See, I have handed Jericho over to you, with its king and the valiant warriors. And you shall march around the city, all the men of war circling the city once a day. You shall do so for six days. Also, seven priests shall carry seven trumpets of rams' horns in front of the ark; then on the seventh day you shall march around the city seven times, and the priests shall blow the trumpets. It shall be that when they make a long blast with the ram's horn, and when you hear the sound of the trumpet, all the people shall shout with a great shout; and the wall of the city will fall down flat, and the people shall go up, everyone straight ahead" (Joshua 6: 1 - 6, NASB). Without hesitancy, Joshua called the priests and told them what God's plan was to defeat Jericho (Joshua 6: 6 - 12, NASB). Joshua was a participatory leader, he did not just relayed God's plans to the Israelites, but he actively participated in carrying them out. Joshua was a good leader. Rahab the prostitute, received favor and kindness from the Israelites marching force because of her kind response when Jericho was being destroyed by the Israelites (Joshua 6: 12 - 17, NASB). The Israelites destroyed everything in Jericho. "... Joshua said to the two men who had spied out the land, go into the prostitute's house and bring the woman and all she has out of there, just as you have sworn to her. So, the young men who were spies went in and brought out Rahab, her father, her mother, her brothers, and all she had; they also brought out all her relatives and placed them outside the camp of Israel. Then they burned the city with fire, and all that was in it. Only the silver and gold, and the articles of bronze and iron, they put into the treasury of the house of the LORD. However, Rahab the prostitute and her father's household and all she had, Joshua spared; and she has lived among the Israelites to this day, because she hid the messengers whom Joshua sent to spy out Jericho. So, the LORD was with Joshua, and his fame was in all the land. (Joshua 6: 22 - 27, NASB). The Israelites were able to conquer Jericho because of Joshua's positive response to the Lord and for following God's plan meticulously. God blessed Joshua for his response and for his faith in Him.

Daniel in the King's Palace in Babylon

Daniel and his friends were part of the captives carried to Babylon as spoils after the defeat of the Israelites. King Nebuchadnezzar chose Daniel (Belteshazzarar), Hananiah (Shadrach), Mishaal (Meshach), and Azariah (Abednego). King Nebuchazzar chose the four Israelites to serve in his palace because of their youthfulness and their perceived ability to learn the culture and the language of the Babylonians. The king decided to treat them as his own and allowed them to eat the royal food and drink the royal wine. The king assigned an official to oversee their diet. However, after observing the type of food and wine being presented to them, they decided that eating such food and drinking such wine would defile them. However, without having the knowledge of what Paul later said they conducted themselves accordingly. "Do not tear down the work of God for the sake of food..." (Romans 14: 20, NASB). Therefore, they made a request with Daniel serving as their spokesperson to the official in charge of their diet that they preferred to eat only vegetables and to drink only water (a vegetarian diet). The official was afraid that they might look different in their physical appearances from other young men who ate the royal food and drank the royal wine and if that should happen, he would be in danger of losing his life. Daniel got into an agreement with the official to give them only ten days on the vegetarian diet and then to evaluate them to see if they were physically inferior to those who were eating the royal food and drinking the royal wine. God gave them favor before the official who granted their request. When they were evaluated after ten days on the vegetarian diet, they looked heathier and better nourished than those on the royal diet (Daniel 1: 3-16 - NASB). The fact that those four young men, Daniel, Hananiah, Mishaal, and Azariah responded to the official with a request of change of diet instead of just going along with eating what other young men were eating. This response set them apart not only among other young men's physical appearances, but with God using them for His purpose from that point onward.

Daniel and the King's Dream

King Nebuchadnezzar had a dream which bothered him a great deal and he could not sleep. He called the magicians, the enchanters, the sorcerers, and the astrologers and he demanded that they tell him his dream and the meaning of his dream. If they were not able to tell him his dream and its meaning, he was going to have them killed. The magicians, the enchanters, the sorcerers, and the astrologer were perplexed and responded to the king that it was too difficult for human beings to know the king's dream and to interpret its meaning. They contended that only the gods which do not live among humans could tell the king his dream and give its meaning. For their response, the king was ready to execute them all. Daniel and his men were included in the execution list. Daniel being aware of the impending doom approached the official who was assigned to oversee the execution of all the wise men in Babylon and appealed to him with wisdom and tact. The official explained the king's demand to Daniel. After understanding the matter, Daniel went to the king himself. Daniel's action as one of those who was on the execution list was commendable, but dangerous. His response to the king was a request of permission for more time to tell the kings dream and to interpret the dream. His response eventually saved him, his comrades, and all the wise men in Babylon. Daniel discussed the matter with his comrades Hananiah, Mishaal, and Azariah and emphasized the importance of actions on their parts to save themselves and all the wise men in Babylon. His response to the king's demand was for him and his comrades to plead for mercy from the God of Heaven. At his urge they all prayed to God for wisdom, and enlightenment. God was merciful unto them and gave Daniel the king's dream and its meaning. Daniel, Hananiah, Mishaal, and Azariah praised God for His intervention on their behalf. Daniel approached the king's official (Arioch) and appealed to him not to kill the wise men in Babylon, but to allow him to speak to the king himself because he had secured the king's dream and its meaning. Daniel was taken to the king who was skeptical that Daniel could do what his trusted older and wiser magicians, enchanters, sorcerers, and astrologers could not do which was revealing the kings dream and interpreting its meaning. Daniel gave credit to God for the revelation of the king's dream. The king was not in any mood for anyone to waste his time any longer and he put this pointed question to Daniel, "Are you able to tell what I saw in my dream and interpret it? (Daniel 2: 26 - NASB). Daniel did not take credit for himself or for his comrades, but to God in his response to the king by saying "No wise man, enchanter, magician or diviner can explain to the king the mystery he has asked about, but there is a God in heaven who reveals mysteries. He has shown King Nebuchadnezzar what will happen in days to come" (Daniel 2; 27 - NASB). Daniel's response to the emerging situation saved him, his comrades and all the wise men in Babylon. In Daniel's response he referred to the king in a third person singular pronoun instead of in the second person singular pronoun. It appears as if he used the techniques to remove the king's personal emotion from the situation and to direct the attention to God. Daniel's response made a difference on the matter of life or death for him, his comrades, and all the wise men of Babylon. Daniel's response saved all those on the execution list. Daniel's response to the situation not only saved all those on the death roll, but it provided recognition of God as being above all gods, Lord of all kings, and a revealer of all mysteries. After his response to the king, Daniel declared the king's dream and revealed its interpretation (Daniel 2: 36 - 45 - NASB). This pagan king through the response of Daniel heaped a huge amount of praise on the true God - the God of Daniel (Daniel 2: 46 - 47 -NASB). The king rewarded Daniel with an elevated position in his kingdom and made him the chief of the wise men in Babylon at his early age. Daniel was also able to secure positions of authority for his comrades as Daniel remained in the Royal Court (Daniel 2: 48 – 49, NASB).

Shadrach, Meshach, and Abednego
in the burning furnace

It was not long after Nebuchadnezzar declared the God of Daniel was God of all gods that he erected a huge golden image.

King nebuchadnezzar had an elaborate dedication ceremony, and he invited all the officials in Babylon. At the ceremony, the king made a decree and commanded all the inhabitants of Babylon to bow down and worship the golden image wherever and whenever they hear the horn, flute, zitther, lyre, harp, pipe, and all kinds of music (Daniel 3: 1 - 6, NASB). Anyone who disobeyed the kings decree was to be tossed into the blazing furnace. However, not long after the king's decree was in effect that some astrologers came forward to the king and reported that some Jews (Shadrach, Meshach, and Abednego) have defiled the king's orders and refused to worship the king's gods and did not bow down to the golden image at the sound of the horn, zither, lyre, harp, pipe, and all kinds of music. Upon hearing that report Nebuchadnezzar was furious with rage and summoned Shadrach, Meshach, and Abednego to his palace and gave them direct command to obey his decree. He threatened them that failure to obey his decree would land them in the blazing furnace and no god could save them from his hand. Shadrach, Meshach, and Abednego at that point had reached the 'fork in the road', and they had to decide and respond to the king. They responded with their trust in God and their deviance of king Nebuchadnezzar's decree. They declared that the God they serve would protect them in the blazing furnace and save them from the hand of Nebuchadnezzar. On the other hand, they responded that even if the God they serve did not save them they have determined not to obey the king's decree. Their response appeared to be an elevated risk taking, especially, since the king was determined to destroy anyone who disobeyed his decree. However, the three, Shadrach, Meshach, and Abednego were not afraid of the consequences which might result from their action and response to the king in an open deviance because they trusted that God would do the best for them. If their response and action resulted in their death or if God saved them, they were sure that God would do what was best for them. Since they trusted God, they were not afraid of the king for the consequences that would follow their response and action. They were ready to accept whatever consequences came their way. Although, Shadrach, Meshach, and Abednego were not aware of what Paul said, "For me, to live is Christ, and to die is gain" (Philippians 1: 21), however, they believed that they did not have anything to lose by following God, but a lot to gain. Therefore, with that mindset they were able to stand up to the powerful king of Babylon.

Shadrach, Meshach, and Abednego in the Fierce Burning Furnace

The consequence came very quick and fierce. Nebuchadnezzar ordered the furnace to be heated seven times hotter than usual. Then the king had them tied up and had them thrown into the furnace with their clothes on them. The soldiers who threw them into the blaze were killed by the heat of the Furnace, but nothing happened to the three.

God did not forget Shadrach, Meshach, and Abednego and their loyalty to Him that He sent an "angel" to accompany them in the furnace. They were all walking around in the furnace without being injured with their clothes still on (Daniel 3: 7 - 25, NASB). This incident showed the character of God as revealed to Isaiah "But now this is what the Lord says - who created you, Jacob, he who formed you, Israel: Do not fear, for I have redeemed you, I have summoned you by name, you are mine. When you pass through the waters, I will be with you; and when you pass through the rivers, they will not sweep over you. When you walk through the fire you will not be burned, the flame will not set you ablaze. For I am the Lord your God, the holy one of Israel, your Savior" (Isaiah 43: 1 - 3, NASB). Shadrach, Meshach, and Abednego were put in the blazing furnace, but they were not burned. God was true to his words, and He protected His own during danger. When Nebuchadnezzar saw God's intervention, he proclaimed the power of God at this second incident (Daniel 3: 26 - 30, NASB). Although Nebuchadnezzar praised God with his mouth, his heart was far from truly embracing the worship of God. God was not pleased with Nebuchadnezzar then and He is still not pleased today when people worship only with their mouth as could be seen in the following passages: "Then the Lord said, "Because this people draw near with their words and honor Me with their lips service, but they remove their hearts far from Me, and their reference for Me consists off the traditions learned by rote" (Isaiah 29: 13, NASB). "And they come to you as people come, and they sit before you as My people, but they do the lustful desires expressed by their mouth, and their heart goes after their gain" (Ezekiel 33: 31, NASB). "You hypocrites, rightly did Isaiah prophesy of you saying, THIS PEOPLE HONOR ME WITH THEIR LIPS, BUT THEIR HEART IS FAR AWAY FROM ME. BUT IN VAIN DO THEY WORSHIP ME TEACHING AS THEIR DOCTRINE THE PRECEPTS OF MEN" (Matthew 15: 7 - 9, NASB). Nebuchadnezzar felt to be deceiving humans by appearing to show allegiance to God by his words of mouth and if he was not intending to deceive humans his believe in God was not deep rooted inside him, but superficial and momentary. It was like the parable Jesus told of the four types of soil on which the seeds fell, especially, the seeds which fell on the rocky soil which grew quickly but had no soil to nurture them and sustain them and they died without yielding any fruit (Matthew 13: 3 - 9, NASB). God was not happy with the hypocrisy of Nebuchadnezzar, and He drove him away to live in the wilderness for seven years where he ate grass like animals. However, when he responded with repentance God was merciful unto him (Daniel 4: 25 - 35, NASB). Human responses to God are not always without reward or punishment from God. God's protection of Shadrach, Meshach, and Abednego from the blazing furnace happened because of their response to the decree of the king and their unwavering trust in God. They trusted God and God did not fail them. King Nebuchadnezzar promoted them again in the province of Babylon.

Daniel in the Den of Lions

Darius, the king, appointed one hundred and twenty (120) Satraps to be over the kingdom of Babylon and over those satraps he chose three commissioners to supervise the satraps. Daniel was one of the commissioners. Daniel exceeded among the commissioners because of an extraordinary spirit in him - the spirit of God. The satraps and other commissioners were jealous of Daniel, especially, after learning that king Darius was intending to appoint him over the entire kingdom. All the officials conspired to find fault against Daniel in the performance of his official government duties. However, when they were not able to find fault against him in his official government duties, they changed their tactics. Knowing that he was a devote follower of God to whom he prayed regularly, they were sure that they could use that practice against him before the king. For their plan to be successful against Daniel they approached the king and advised him to make a decree, an injunction and to sign it that no one under Darius' kingdom could consult with any god or man for thirty days except with the king only. They had the king agree with their scheme and the king signed an injunction with the punishment that whoever disobeyed the decree would be thrown into the den of lion. As his customary practice Daniel continued to pray to God three times a day. The perpetrators went to Daniel's house and found him praying to God. They then went with the evidence to the king proving that Daniel disobeyed the king's decree/injunction/verdict and that he should be thrown into the den of lions. The king was bordered by the thought that he would have to throw Daniel, an innocent person into the den of lions. However, because of his response to the scheme of the satraps, the commissioners, and the governors who persuaded him to sign a decree he had no choice but to go against his own wish by throwing Daniel into the den of lions. He encouraged Daniel before ordering him to be thrown into the den of lions "Your God whom you constantly serve will

Himself deliver you" (Daniel 6: 16, NASB). The king regretted that he signed a decree and that there was no turning back from the consequence of his response of signing the decree. The lesson from this incident is that there could be consequence(s) to a person's response(s) to issues. Darius went to his palace, but he was not able to sleep because he realized that Daniel had not done any wrong and if Daniel was to be killed by the lions it was him who had shed the blood of an innocent man. Reeling from his guilty feeling, he rose early in the morning hoping for the best that the lions, somehow, did not kill Daniel, but being pragmatic that the chance of Daniel being alive was very slim. On his way to the den of lions many thoughts must have been flowing through his mind, he might be afraid of what he might see, the bloody clothes of Daniel, pieces of Daniel's flesh thrown all over the den, and/or the sprinkles of Daniel's blood splattered all over the wall of the den of lions. As he was getting closer to the den of lions where Daniel was thrown his feelings were not very comforting to him and his guiltiness must have overtaken him, and he must have felt like a 'dead man' walking. At the entrance of the den of lions, he put up the last courage and called the name of Daniel, wishing deeply inside him that he would get an answer. He was not courageous enough at that point to look down into the den of lions for the fear of what he might see or might not see.

With fear and trepidation, king Darius called out to Daniel and said, "Daniel, servant of the living God, has your God, whom you constantly serve, been able to deliver you from the lions? Daniel

91

responded to the king with no resentment, but he said, O king, live forever! My God sent His angel and shut the lions' mouths and they have not harmed me, in as much as I was found innocent before Him; and also, toward you, O king." (Daniel 6: 21 - 22, NASB). Daniel's response after the mistreatment he had received was not of resentment or of vengeance, but of offering of prayer for the king's long life. Daniel made it known to king Darius that God protected him because of his innocence to the king and of his commitment to serving God. Daniel's response was the greatest witness to the king. After the king ordered Daniel to be fetched out of the den of lions, he made the following declarations to his entire kingdom. The king then gave orders, and they brought those men who had deceived the king to sign a decree and who had maliciously accused Daniel, and they cast them, their children, and their wives into the lions' den; and they had not reached the bottom of the den before the lions overpowered them and crushed all their bones. "Then Darius the king wrote to all the peoples, nations, and men of every language who were living in all the land: May your peace abound! I make a decree that in all the dominion of my kingdom men are to fear and tremble before the God of Daniel; For He is the living God and enduring forever, And His kingdom is one which will not be destroyed, And His dominion will be forever. He delivers and rescues and performs signs and wonders. In heaven and on earth, Who has also delivered Daniel from the power of the lions. So, this Daniel enjoyed success in the reign of Darius and in the reign of Cyrus the Persian" (Daniel 6: 1 - 28, NASB).

Saul's Response and the loss of his Kingship

When things do not go as one expects it is important to be careful with one's response to the situation. Things do not always go as one plans, but one should be flexible enough to adjust to the unplanned situation and ask for God's direction. However, this was not the response of Saul. "As for Saul, he was still in Gilgal, and all the people followed him trembling. Then he waited seven days, according to the time set by Samuel. But Samuel did not come to Gilgal; and the people were scattered from him. So, Saul said, "Bring a burnt offering and peace offerings here to me. And he offered the burnt offering. Now it happened, as soon as he had finished presenting the burnt offering, that Samuel came; and Saul went out to meet him, that he might greet him. And Samuel said, What have you done? Saul said, When I saw that the people were scattered from me, and that you did not come within the days appointed, and that the Philistines gathered at Michmash, then I said, The Philistines will now come down on me at Gilgal, and I have not made supplication to the LORD Therefore, I felt compelled, and offered a burnt offering. And Samuel said to Saul, You have done foolishly. You have not kept the commandment of the LORD your God, which He commanded you. For now, the LORD would have established your kingdom over Israel forever. But now your kingdom shall not continue. The LORD has sought for Himself a man after His own heart, and the LORD has commanded him to be commander over His people, because you have not kept what the LORD commanded you." (1 Samuel 13: 7 - 14, NASB).

The response of Saul destroyed the relationship between him and God with the consequence of a shortened kingship. The role of Saul was to rule and lead the people and the role of Samuel was to represent the people before God and to serve as their mediator by offering sacrifices to God on their behalf and that was not the role of Saul. How Saul responded impatiently to delay in Samuel's arrival in Gilgal to perform the sacrifice and he (Saul) usurp the position of the priest. Therefore, God shortened his kingship and removed His spirit from him. Responses have consequences good or bad, therefore, it is important that one allows God to always direct one's responses.

David and Saul

"Now the Spirit of the LORD left Saul, and an evil spirit from the LORD terrified him. Saul's servants then said to him, "Behold now, an evil spirit from God is terrifying you. May our lord now command your servants who are before you. Have them search for a man who is a skillful musician on the harp; and it shall come about whenever the evil spirit from God is upon you, that he shall play the harp with his hand, and you will become well. So, Saul said to his servants, Now, select for me a man who can play well and bring him to me. Then one of the young men responded and said, "Behold, I have seen a son of Jesse the Bethlehemite who is a skillful musician, a valiant mighty man, a warrior, skillful in speech, and a handsome man; and the LORD is with him. So, Saul sent messengers to Jesse to say, Send me your son David, who is with the flock. And Jesse took a donkey loaded with bread and a jug of wine, and he took a young goat, and sent them to Saul by his son David. Then David came to Saul and attended to him; and Saul loved him, and he became his armor bearer. So, Saul sent word to Jesse, saying, Let David now be my attendant for he has found favor in my sight. So, it came about whenever the evil spirit from God came to Saul, David would take the harp and play it with his hand; and Saul would feel relieved and become well, and the evil spirit would leave him." (1 Samuel 16: 14- 23, NASB). Although David was playing music to calm Saul down and to improve his welfare Saul's response constantly was to kill him. Saul was so jealous of David that his constant intent was to kill him. Despite Saul's response David was always ready to attend to Saul to play music for him in order to improve his welfare. The situation got worse that David had to flee for his life to the wilderness of Ziph, at Horesh. "Now David and his men were in the wilderness of Moan, in the Arabah to the south of Jeshimon. When Saul and his men went to seek him, they informed David, and he came down to the rock and stayed in the wilderness of Moan. And when Saul heard about it, he pursued David in the wilderness of Moan. Saul went on one side of the mountain, and David and his men on the other side of the mountain; and David was hurrying to get away from Saul, while Saul and his men were surrounding David and his men to apprehend them. But a messenger came to Saul, saying, Hurry and come, for the Philistines have launched an attack against the land! So, Saul returned from pursuing David and Nathan" (1 Samuel 23: 24 - 28, NASB). God's divine intervention was fulfilled with the incident of the Philistines invading the land which made Saul abandon his pursuit of David, at least, temporarily.

David had moved to the wilderness of Enged when Saul returned from pursuing the Philistines, Saul with three thousand chosen men from all Israel renewed his pursuit of David. During his pursuit of David, he found a cave on the way and Saul went in to relieve himself. David and his men were sitting in the inner recesses of the same cave. David's men urged him to take the unique opportunity afforded him to kill Saul. David had a choice to do to Saul as it seemed good to him. In response to the advice of his men David decided to spare the life of Saul when he had the opportunity to kill Saul, his enemy. Instead of killing Saul he cut off the edge of Saul's robe secretly. However, only for cutting off the edge of Saul's robe David's conscience bothered him. David regretted that he did such a thing to the anointed of God. David acknowledged Saul as his lord. David forbade his men from attacking Saul. Saul was oblivious to what had happened while he was in the cave. After Saul had left the cave David wanted him to be aware that he had the opportunity to harm him, but he refrained from doing so. David still responded to Saul as the king who deserved his respect and David bowed with his face to the ground and prostrated himself. David said to Saul, "Why do you listen to the words of men who say, 'Behold, David is seeking to harm you'? Behold, this day your eyes have seen that the LORD had handed you over to me today in the cave, and someone said to kill you, but I spared you; and I said, 'I will not reach out with my hand against my lord, because he is the LORD'S anointed.' So, my father, look! Indeed, look at the edge of your robe in my hand! For by the fact that I cut off the edge of your robe but did not kill you, know and understand that there is no evil or rebellion in my hands, and I have not sinned against you, though you are lying in wait for my life, to take it. May the LORD judge between you and me, and may the LORD take vengeance on you for me; but my hand shall not be against you. As the proverb of the ancients says, 'Out of the wicked comes wickedness; but my hand shall not be against you. After whom has the king of Israel gone out? Whom are you pursuing? A dead dog, a single flea? May the LORD therefore be judge and decide between you and me; and may He see and plead my cause and save me from your hand" (1 Samuel 24; 1 - 15, NASB).

"After Saul realized how David was so kind to him, he regretted his dealings with David and acknowledged how wickedly he had dealt with David and how David did not pay him back according to his (Saul's) wickedness towards David. Saul said, Is this your voice, my son David? Then Saul raised his voice and wept. And he said to David, you are more righteous than I; for you have dealt well with me, while I have dealt maliciously with you. You have declared today that you have done good to me, that the LORD handed me over to you and yet you did not kill me. Though if a man finds his enemy, will he let him go away unharmed? May the LORD therefore reward you with good in return for what you have done to me this day. Now, behold, I know that you will certainly be king, and that the kingdom of Israel will be established in your hand. So now swear to me by the LORD that you will not cut off my descendants after me, and that you will not eliminate my name from my father's household. And David swore an oath to Saul. Then Saul went to his home, but David and his men went up to the stronghold" (1 Samuel 24: 16 - 22, NASB). As a result of David's responses and treatment of Saul there was peace agreement signed between them, however, David did not have full trust of Saul, therefore, David and his men went for protection in a safe place. When Saul was caught 'flat-footed' he shed 'crocodile tears.' Saul's insincerity was palpable with his hypocrisy. When a person is caught in wrongdoing, and he/she begins to weep there could be one of two reasons for the weeping. First, the person could be weeping as a true remorse for the wrong done. The weeping could also be a result of regret, guiltiness, or repentance. Second, the weeping could be because the person is caught, and he/she is not able to get away with the wrongdoing and he/she is overtaking with shame of being caught but such weeping is not of true repentance, guilt, or sorrowfulness for the wrong done. Saul's weeping was not born out of regret or repentance but of a pretense and it was fake. Saul's deceitful regret or repentance for how he had treated David did not last long. Saul's response of rage, anger, jealousy, and hatred towards David soon returned to him. When a report came to Saul of the location of where David and his men were taking refuge Saul in disregard to his prior regret and repentance for treating David wickedly decided to pursue David again in order to destroy him. Saul's words were vain words which did not match his actions for he said one thing and did the opposite when it came to his treatment of David. "So, Saul set out and went down to the wilderness of Ziph, taking with him three thousand chosen men of Israel to search for David in the wilderness of Ziph. And Saul camped on the hill of Hachilah, which is opposite Jeshimon, beside the road, and David was staying in the wilderness. When he saw that Saul had come after him into the wilderness, David sent out spies, and he learned that Saul was coming. David then set out and came to the place where Saul had camped. And David saw the place where Saul lay, and Abner the son of Ner, the commander of his army; and Saul was lying in the circle of the camp, and the people were camped around him. Then David said to Ahimelech the Hittite and to Abishai the son of Zeruiah, Joab's brother, saying, who will go down with me to Saul in the camp? And Abishai said, I will go down with you. So, David and Abishai came to the people by night, and behold, Saul lay sleeping inside the circle of the camp with his spear stuck in the ground at his head; and Abner and the people were lying around him. Then Abishai said to David, Today God has handed your enemy over to you; now then, please let me pin him with the spear to the ground with one thrust, and I will not do it to him a second time. But David said to Abishai, Do not kill him, for who can reach out with his hand against the Lord's anointed and remain innocent? David also said, as the LORD lives, the LORD certainly will strike him, or his day will come that he dies, or he will go down in battle and perish. The Lord forbid that I would reach out with my hand against the Lord's anointed! But now please take the spear that is at his head and the jug of water and let us go. So, David took the spear and the jug of water that were at Saul's head, and they left; and no one saw or knew about it, nor did anyone awaken, for they were all asleep, because a deep sleep from the LORD had fallen on them. Then David crossed over to the other side and stood on top of the mountain at a distance with a large area between them. And David called to the people and to Abner the son of Ner, saying, Will you not answer, Abner? Then Abner replied, who are you who calls to the king? So, David said to Abner, are you not a man? And who is like you in Israel? Why then have you not guarded your lord the king? For one of the people came to kill the king your lord! This thing that you have done is not good. As the LORD lives, all of you undoubtedly must die, because you did not guard your lord, the Lord's anointed. And now, see where the king's spear is and the jug of water that was at his head! Then Saul recognized David's voice and said, Is this your voice, my son David? And David said, it is my voice, my lord the king. He also said, why then is my lord pursuing his servant? For what have I done? Or what evil is in my hand? Now then, please let my lord the king listen to the words of his servant. If the LORD has incited you against me, may He accept an offering; but if it is people, cursed are they before he LORD, because they have driven me out today so that I would have no share in the inheritance of the LORD, saying, Go, serve other gods. Now then, do not let my blood fall to the ground far from the presence of the LORD; for the king of Israel has come out to search for a single flea, just as one hunts a partridge in the mountains Then Saul said, I have sinned. Return, my son David, for I will not harm you again since my life was precious in your sight this day. Behold, I have played the fool and have made a very great mistake. David replied, behold, the spear of the king! Now have one of the young men come over and take it. And the LORD will repay each man for his righteousness and his faithfulness; for the LORD handed you over to me today, but I refused to reach out with my hand against the Lord's anointed. Therefore behold, just as your life was highly valued in my sight this day, so may my life be highly valued in the sight of the LORD, and may He rescue me from all distress. Then Saul said to David, blessed are you, my son David; you will both accomplish much and assuredly prevail. So, David went on his way, and Saul returned to his place"

(1 Samuel 26: 2 - 25, NASB). The incident above was the second time when David was handed the opportunity to kill Saul, but David's response was to refuse to take advantage of the opportunities afforded him to kill his enemy, Saul. Instead of killing Saul he feared God and he refused to be responsible for killing the Lord's anointed. In this incident as in the previous one of his men advised him to make the best of his advantage over Saul to kill him. His men even volunteered to be the ones to kill Saul, but he forbade them. His response was based on his reference to God with the believe that if God wanted to kill Saul it would not be through his hands or through his participation, but through the hands of others. Whenever Saul was caught, and David spared his life he always produced phony appearance of his loyalty to David who he was pursuing to kill. With the narcissistic tendencies of Saul, all he could think was anything to benefit him or to 'safe his skin.' Saul was ready to say or do anything whenever he was cornered or caught with his hands in the 'cookie jar,' he would look for a way to get out of the situation even if that meant having words coming out of his mouth which he did not mean. Saul was self-centered and phony in his declarations. Although David was aware of those character defects of Saul, his response was to maintain his loyalty to God and not to pay Saul evil for the evil which Saul wished for him. As a result of David's loyalty to God, God continued to protect him from the evil schemes of Saul, and he was always having upper hand on Saul. David was faithful to God in his responses to Saul and God remained faithful to him and kept him safe. However, David being keenly aware that Saul could not be trusted decided not to take a chance with his life, therefore, he decided to flee to the land of the Philistines to keep himself away from the reach of Saul in Israel. "Then David said to himself, now I will perish one day by the hand of Saul. There is nothing better for me than to safely escape into the land of the Philistines. Then Saul will despair of searching for me anymore in all the territory of Israel, and I will escape from his hand. So, David set out and went over, he and the six hundred men who were with him, to Achish the son of Maoch, king of Gath. And David lived with Achish in Gath, he, and his men, each with his own household - David with his two wives, Ahinoam the Jezreelitess, and Abigail the Carmelitess, Nabal's

widow. Now it was reported to Saul that David had fled to Gath, so he no longer searched for him" (1 Samuel 27: 1- 4, NASB).

Nathan Confronted David

Although David had had his eyes on the Lord and following God, however, when he went up to the top of the roof of his house, he lifted his eyes off the Lord and shifted his attention to the bathing woman. In David's response he kept his eyes on the wife of another man, Uriah, one of his soldiers. David was so tempted by lust that he had, Bethsheba, the wife of another man brought to his house/palace where he committed adultery with her. David intention was only to commit adultery with a married woman and to let her go without anyone knowing what had happened between them, but David's sin caught up with him in that the woman got pregnant while the husband was at war protecting the kingdom of David. What David did in secrete became revealed in the open and David had nowhere to hide from his sin as he was aware that the growth of his sin would be apparent to all who saw the woman as her belly continues to grow without her husband being around. This occurrence was congruent with the statement in the gospel of Luke and the gospel of Mark, "For nothing is concealed that will not become evident, nor anything hidden that will not be known and come to light" (Luke 8: 17, NASB). "For nothing is hidden, except to be revealed; nor has anything been secret, but that it would come to light" (Mark 4: 22, NASB). David made up all sorts of schemes to hide his sin, but they all failed, and he eventually planned the last scheme which killed Uriah. "Now at evening time David got up from his bed and walked around on the roof of the king's house, and from the roof he saw a woman bathing; and the woman was incredibly beautiful in appearance. So, David sent servants and inquired about the woman. And someone said, Is this not Bathsheba, the daughter of Eliam, the wife of Uriah the Hittite? Then David sent messengers and had her brought, and when she came to him, he slept with her; and when she had purified herself from her uncleanness, she returned to her house. But the woman conceived; so, she sent word and informed David, and said, I am pregnant. Then David sent word to Joab: Send me Uriah the Hittite. So, Joab sent Uriah to David. When Uriah came to him, David asked about Joab's well-being and that of the people, and the condition of the war. Then David said to Uriah, go down to your house, and wash your feet. So, Uriah left the king's house, and a gift from the king was sent after him. But Uriah slept at the door of the king's house with all the servants of his lord and did not go down to his house. Now when they informed David, saying, Uriah did not go down to his house, David said to Uriah, did you not come from a journey? Why did you not go down to your house? And Uriah said to David, the ark and Israel and Judah are staying in temporary shelters, and my lord Joab and the servants of my lord are camping in the open field. Should I then go to my house to eat and drink and to sleep with my wife? By your life and the life of your soul, I will not do this thing. Then, David said to Uriah, stay here today also, and tomorrow I will let you go back. So, Uriah remained in Jerusalem that day and the day after. Now David summoned Uriah, and he ate and drank in his presence, and he made Uriah drunk; and in the evening Uriah went out to lie on his bed with his lord's servants, and he still did not go down to his house. So, in the morning David wrote a letter to Joab and sent it by the hand of Uriah. He had written in the letter the following: Station Uriah on the front line of the fiercest battle and pull back from him, so that he may be struck and killed. So, it was as Joab kept watch on the city, that he stationed Uriah at the place where he knew there were valiant men. And the men of the city went out and fought against Joab, and some of the people among David's servants fell; and Uriah the Hittite also died. Then Joab sent a messenger and reported to David all the events of the war" (2 Samuel 11: 2 - 18, NASB). " When the time of mourning was over, David sent servants and had her brought to his house and she became his wife; then she bore him a son. But the thing that David had done was evil in the sight of the LORD" (2 Samuel 11: 27, NASB). It is always easy for an individual to condemn others and to prescribe harsh punishment for others before knowing the details of the matter. This was the case with David in his response to Nathan. He felt self-righteous to pass judgement on others without showing any mercy. Because of his harsh response and determination for harsh treatment

103

for others he was humbled and humiliated when Nathan declared to him that he was really the one of whom he was referring. David's response was of remorse, repentance, and a request for forgiveness from the Lord. David realized that his heart was unclean and that his spirit was not steady with God, he knew that the only solution to his problem was for God to give him a spirit and a heart transplant. David did not give any excuse for his sinfulness, and he acknowledged that he knew better the will of God even from his mother's womb and there was no excuses for the sin he committed. David realized that he needed God presence in his life through the Holy Spirit , but he realized that the Holy Spirit could not abide with him due to his sinfulness, therefore, he appealed to God to retain His Holy Spirit within him and not to withdraw His Holy Spirit from him. Therefore, he asked God to create in him a clean heart and to renew a steadfast spirit within him (Psalm 51: 1 - 19, NASB). David realized that his problem was his heart, and he was appealing to God for a new heart. David realized that his action was wicked and that his heart deceived him. As stated in Jeremiah, "The heart is deceitful above all things and desperately wicked; Who can know it? I, the LORD, search the heart, I test the mind, even to give every man according to his ways, according to the fruit of his doings (Jeremiah 17: 9 – 10, NKJV). David knew the consequences which could come to him as a result of his sin, therefore he repented and asked for forgiveness from God. As a result of his repentance God preserved his life, but not the life of the son born to him in adultery. Even though God forgave him because of his response the consequences of his sin lingered in his family in form of feuds and the rise of evils within his family. Then the LORD sent Nathan to David. And he came to him and said, there were two men in a city, the one wealthy and the other poor. The wealthy man had a great many flocks and herds. But the poor man had nothing at all except one little ewe lamb which he bought and nurtured; And it grew up together with him and his children. It would eat scraps from him and drink from his cup and lie in his lap and was like a daughter to him. Now a visitor came to the wealthy man, and he could not bring himself to take any animal from his own flock or his own herd to prepare for the traveler who had come to him. So, he took the poor man's ewe lamb and prepared it for the man who had come to him. Then David's anger burned against the man, and he said to Nathan, as the LORD lives, the man who has done this certainly deserves to die! So, he must make restitution for the lamb four times over since he did this thing and had no compassion. Nathan then said to David, you yourself are the man! This is what the LORD, the God of Israel says: 'It is I who anointed you as king over Israel, and it is I who rescued you from the hand of Saul. I also gave you your master's house and put your master's wives into your care, and I gave you the house of Israel and Judah; and if that had been too little, I would have added to you many more things like these! Why have you despised the word of the LORD, by doing evil in His sight? You have struck and killed Uriah the Hittite with the sword, you have taken his wife as your wife, and you have slaughtered him with the sword of the sons of Ammon. Now then, the sword shall never leave your house, because you have despised Me and have taken the wife of Uriah the Hittite to be your wife. This is what the LORD says: Behold, I am going to raise up evil against you from your own household; I will even take your wives before your eyes and give them to your companion, and he will sleep with your wives in broad daylight. Indeed, you did it secretly, but I will do this thing before all Israel, and in open daylight. Then David said to Nathan, I have sinned against the LORD. And Nathan said to David, The LORD also has allowed your sin to pass; you shall not die. However, since by this deed you have shown utter disrespect for the LORD, the child himself who is born to you shall certainly die" (2 Samuel 12: 2 - 14, NASB

David's Response to the Return of the Ark of Covenant

David went from Baale-judah, with all the people who were with him, to bring up the Ark of Covenant to Jerusalem.

However, the Ark of Covenant was not brought directly to Jerusalem. But it was diverted to the house of Obed-Edom because one of the people moving the ark touched it and he died as a punishment for touching the ark. Therefore, David was afraid and diverted the ark to the home of Obed-Edom. Obed-Edom and his household were blessed because of the presence of the ark of the Lord in his home. When David heard of the blessings Obed-Edom was receiving from the Lord he decided to move the ark to its intended destination in Jerusalem. They were able to move the Ark of Covenant to Jerusalem without any bad incident.

David was incredibly happy and elated with the accomplishment that he began to dance before the Lord, and he blessed the people. In praise of the Lord, he danced publicly in front of all the people. When his wife, Michal, saw him dancing in public with the Israelites she was disgusted with David's action. David was dancing as a praise to

the Lord who made it possible for them to bring the Ark of the Lord back to Jerusalem. But his wife felt that he debased himself before the people. When David arrived at the palace to bless his own family, his wife interrupted him and showed her unhappiness with him for dancing shamelessly in public. In her response she cared more about David's appearance before humans than David's praise of the Lord. Michal was more concerned that David's behavior had a reflection on her before the people. She was more concerned about her own image than the openness in worshipping the Lord, therefore, she rebuked David. In fact, she obstructed the plan of David to bless his family just as he blessed the Israelites. In response, David rebuked his wife and she remained barren throughout her life. For David's joyous response for the return of the ark of the Lord, God accepted him. However, for the response of Michal, she remained barren throughout her lifetime. (2 Samuel 6: 1 - 23, NASB).

Hannah's Response

Elikanah had two wives: Hannah and Peninnah. Hannah was the favorite wife of Elkanah out of his two wives. However, Hannah was baren, but Peninnah had children. Peninnah provoked Hannah bitterly to irritate her because she was baren and she had children. Elikannah went year after year up to the house of the Lord with his family and even there Peninnah provoked her, therefore, Hannah wept and did not eat. Elikanah tried to comfort her with good words, and he made her know that although she did not have any child, he was more than a child to her. He assured her that she had his unwavering support. Regardless of whatever her husband did it did not remove her sadness. She managed to eat and drink before going to the house of the Lord in one of their voyages. She was so overwhelmed by her sorrow and distress that she could not get herself to pray out loudly, probably because she did not want all those around her, especially, Peninnah to hear her petition to the Lord. Although she was not vocal in her petition to the Lord, her lips were quivering, therefore, Eli, the priest perceived that she was drunk. Eli in his perception challenged Hannah to quit drinking, to be sober and to stop behaving like a drunk. Hannah was polite in her response to Eli, the priest, and she calmly defended her reputation convincingly by letting the priest know that she was not drunk at all and that she was not like other women, but that she was a woman of good reputation. She emphasized to the priest that her heart was worried about her lack of children. She said that she was pleading to the Lord earnestly to provide her a child and that was the reason for her being so overwhelmed by emotion in her petition to the Lord and that she was not drunk. She continued in her response to Eli by emphasizing that she was not asking for a son for selfish reasons, but she would dedicate the son to the work of the Lord all the days of his life and a razor shall never come on his head. The Lord was merciful unto Hannah and provided her with a son who they named

Samuel and they worshiped and dedicated him to the service of the Lord. Hannah reminded Eli the priest of the time she was praying to the Lord and Eli perceived her to be a drunk. She wanted Eli to know that the Lord had answered her petition by giving her the son for which she prayed and in order to fulfil her commitment to the Lord as she promised she had brought him to be dedicated to the Lord. (1 Samuel 13: 1 – 27, NASB). Hannah was commendable in her responses and how she handled her situation with the lack of children, the torturing by Peninnal, and the wrong perception she suffered from Eli who assumed that she was a drunk. Regarding the torturing she received from Peninnal, there was no record that Hannah repaid Peninnah evil for the wrong she had, repeatedly, done to her, but instead she focused her attention on the Lord who she believed could take care of her need for a son. Hannah did not allow her emotional upheavals to prevent her from seeking the Lord for help. However, a place which she believed to be a place of refuge and solace from the torture from Peninnah turned out to be where she got accused of being a drunk by the priest who was supposed to understand her condition and serve as a shield for her or at least to ask question to find out what was happening to her before jumping into a conclusion and instead outright accused her of being a drunk. Hannah handled herself honorably by explaining calmly to Eli, the priest. One lesson which should stand out vividly to the readers is that in any human relationship it is important to find out the facts instead of acting on assumption which might be wrong and because each case could have a different twist to it. Eli acted on assumption and he was wrong, but Hannah was gracious in her response to Eli and she calmly explained her plight. The Lord was merciful unto Hannah and gave her a son which she requested. Hannah's responses made a difference with Peninnal, Eli, and with the Lord.

Consequences of Rehoboam's Response

After the death of Solomon Rehoboam, his son, was in line to be the king over all the twelve tribes of Israel. However, there was another man, Jeroboam, who wanted to be king of Israel, as well. He went into exile while Solomon was king and was waiting for the opportunity to return and contest for kingship when time was appropriate. Rehoboam went to Shechem to meet all Israel. Jeroboam, also, went to Shechem. This meeting was equivalent to a job interview for Rehoboam. As a job interview everything, requests, questions, or demands which came out of the meeting was to be managed with careful considerations and they were not to be taken for granted, especially, with another candidate, Jeroboam, in the waiting. Rehoboam's response to the Israelites in that meeting was, especially, important and the answers should be reasonable. Unlike any regular job interview, Rehoboam knew the questions and the background behind the questions ahead of when he was to provide the answers to the questions and requests posed to him. He could consult with anyone of his choice to get an answer to their questions. Rehoboam took advantage of the opportunity and bought himself three days to produce acceptable answers. In his preparation for an answer, he consulted with the experienced elders who had worked for Solomon, his father. The request from the Israelites was that while Solomon was king, he ruled them with heavy yoke, and they would like Rehoboam to promise to lighten their yoke and to give them assurance that he would lighten their yoke. In return they also assured him that they would always serve him if he promised to lighten their yoke. The elders who had served Solomon gave Rehoboam a wise piece of advice. They made clear to him that in order to be the leader of the people he needed to be their servant. As their servant he needed to listen and consider their concerns carefully. They advised Rehoboam to speak pleasantly to the people and to grant their request. They emphasized that if Rehoboam followed their pieces of advice the people would always serve him. In order to get the job for which he was interviewing which was to be the king of all the twelve tribes of Israel he needed to answer them positively. It is important to weigh the pieces of advice of two groups to know which could be beneficial and which could not. It was very important and beneficial for Rehoboam to have listened to the elders based on their life experiences on handling issues. David, the grandfather of Rehoboam, the king of Israel had some pieces of advice in the book of Psalm which Rehoboam failed to follow. "Blessed is the person who does not walk in the counsel of the wicked, Nor stand in the path of sinners, Nor sit in the seat of scoffers!" (Psalm 1: 1, NASB).

Not only did Rehoboam not listen to the pieces of advice of his grandfather, but he did not also listen to the pieces of advice from his father, Solomon, the son of David, and the king of Israel, in the book of Proverbs, as well. Solomon said, "Where there is no guidance the people fall, But in an abundance of counselors there is victory" (Proverbs 11: 14, NASB). "The way of a fool is right in his own eyes, But a person who listens to advice is wise" (Proverbs 12: 15, NASB).

After hearing the pieces of advice of the experienced wise elders who served his father well, he decided to consult with the young inexperienced men of his age for advice. The elders were accustomed to dealing with the Israelites and they knew how to get things done with them. However, the inexperienced young men instead of calming the situation gave Rehoboam pieces of advice which made the situation worse and alienated the Israelites. They advised Rehoboam to respond to the people harshly and to let them know that he would increase their yoke instead of lightening it. In Rehoboam's response to the Israelites, he discarded the wise pieces of advice of the elders, but followed the wrong pieces of advice of the inexperienced young men.

The consequence of his unwise response to the Israelites was the feelings of alienation by the Israelites and the feelings of not belonging. They all returned to their homes and to their tribes. Rehoboam, because of his response failed to get the job of becoming the king of a unified Israel. Just as in a job interview, one's response has consequence, and it could make a difference in the result as it did for Rehoboam.

"Then Rehoboam went to Shechem because all Israel had come to Shechem to make him king. Now when Jeroboam the son of Nebat heard about this, he was living in Egypt (for he was still in Egypt, where he had fled from the presence of King Solomon). Then they sent word and summoned him, and Jeroboam and all the assembly of Israel came and spoke to Rehoboam, saying, your father made our yoke hard; but now, lighten the hard labor imposed by your father and his heavy yoke which he put on us, and we will serve you. Then he said to them, depart for three days, then return to me. So, the people departed. And King Rehoboam consulted with the elders who had served his father Solomon while he was still alive, saying, how do you advise me to answer this people? Then they spoke to him, saying, if you will be a servant to this people today, and will serve them and grant them their request, and speak pleasant words to them, then they will be your servants always. But he ignored the advice of the elders which they had given him and consulted with the young men who had grown up with him and served him. He said to them, what advice do you give, so that we may answer this people who have spoken to me, saying, Lighten the yoke which your father put on us'? And the young men who had grown up with him spoke to him, saying, this is what you should say to this people who spoke to you, saying: Your father made our yoke heavy, now you make it lighter for us! You should speak this way to them: My little finger is thicker than my father's waist! Now then, my father loaded you with a heavy yoke; yet I will add to your yoke. My father disciplined you with whips, but I will discipline you with scorpions! Then Jeroboam and all the people came to Rehoboam on the third day, just as the king had directed, saying, Return to me on the third day. And the king answered the people harshly, for he ignored the advice of the elders which they had given him, and he spoke to them according to the advice of the young men, saying, My father made your yoke heavy, but I will add to your yoke; my father disciplined you with whips, but I will discipline you with scorpions! So, the king did not listen to the people; because it was a turn of events from the LORD, in order to establish His word which, the LORD spoke through Ahijah the Shilonite to Jeroboam the son of Nebat. When all Israel saw that the king had not listened to them, the people replied to the king, saying, what share do we have in David? We have no inheritance in the son of Jesse, To your tents, Israel! Now look after your own house, David! So, Israel went away to their tents. But as for the sons of Israel who lived in the cities of Judah, Rehoboam reigned over them. (1 KING 12: 1 - 19. NASB). As could be seen with Rehoboam disregarding the pieces of advice from the elders he walked in the counsel of the wicked, he stood in the path of sinners, and he sat in the seat of scoffers which was in direct opposite to what his grandfather advised. Rehoboam even ignored the pieces of advice from his father. He had guidance, counselors, and advisers, but he acted foolishly by not following any of their pieces of advice in his response. The consequences of his response was total failure in becoming the king of the twelve tribes of Israel.

Effects of Ruth's Response to the Tragedy in Her Life

"Then Elimelech, Naomi's husband, died; and she was left with her two sons. And they took for themselves Moabite women as wives; the name of the one was Orpah, and the name of the other, Ruth. And they lived there about ten years. Then both Mahlon and Chilion also died, and the woman was left without her two sons and her husband Then she arose with her daughters-in-law to return from the land of Moab, because she had heard in the land of Moab that the LORD had visited His people by giving them food. So, she departed from the place where she was, and her two daughters-in-law with her; and they went on the way to return to the land of Judah. But Naomi said to her two daughters-in-law, Go, return each of you to your mother's house. May the LORD deal kindly with you as you have dealt with the dead and with me. May the LORD grant that you may find a place of rest, each one in the house of her husband. Then she kissed them, and they raised their voices and wept. However, they said to her, no, but we will return with you to your people. But Naomi said, Return, my daughters. Why should you go with me? Do I still have sons in my womb, that they may be your husbands? Return, my daughters! Go, for I am too old to have a husband. If I said I have hope, if I were even to have a husband tonight and give birth to sons, would you therefore wait until they were grown? Would you therefore refrain from marrying? No, my daughters; for it is much more bitter for me than for you, because the hand of the LORD has come out against me. And they raised their voices and wept again; and Orpah kissed her mother-in-law, but Ruth clung to her. Then she said, Behold, your sister-in-law has gone back to her people and her gods; return after your sister-in-law. But Ruth said, do not plead with me to leave you or to turn back from following you; for where you go, I will go, and where you sleep, I will sleep. Your people shall be my people, and your God, my God. Where you die, I will die, and there I will be buried. May the LORD do so to me, and worse, if anything but death separates me from you When she saw that she was determined to go with her, she stopped speaking to her about it. So, they both went on until they came to Bethlehem" (Ruth 1: 3 - 19, NASB).

Naomi was a widow with two sons, they moved to the land of Moab because of a famine in their homeland in Judah. Her sons got married to two Moabite women, Ruth and Orpah. Both sons died during their time in Moab. Naomi felt that both women were young enough for each to go and each remarry to other man in their homeland. Therefore, she called them to a conference and encouraged them to leave her and go their own way and remarry while she would return to her home country. They all felt sad, hugged, and cried on each other's shoulders. They both refused to leave Naomi by herself. However, Naomi was considerate of her daughters-in-law, and she wanted the best for them, therefore, she insisted that they leave her and to start a new life of their own. She wanted them to leave, to go and remarry and raise families of their own as it was impossible for her to have other sons to marry them. After much persuasion Orpah decided and left Naomi, but Ruth decided and stayed with Naomi. Her response came from her loyalty to Ruth and to the relationship they had formed. She did not want to abandon Naomi. Ruth responded in this manner because she was not thinking of her own welfare, but of the welfare of Naomi. She must have been thinking that she was the only one who Naomi had after the death of her husband and her two sons. She did not think it to be the right thing to abandon Naomi at the time that she needed her most, therefore, she stayed with Naomi.

The more Naomi encouraged her to leave, the more she responded with a determination to stay with her. Ruth was very emphatic when she told Naomi that only death could separate them. At that point Naomi accepted the decision of Ruth to stay and go with her. Ruth put the tragedies which had occurred in her life and in Naomi's life behind them and decided to provide for the sustenance of Naomi and of herself. She did not have the qualifications and the skills needed to get a profitable job in the new land, but she decided that she could harvest the grain left behind in the field.

God was merciful unto her and directed her to the field of Boaz, a relative of Naomi's husband. God blessed Ruth in this manner because of her positive response to the tragedy in her life and in the life of her mother-in-law and for her loyalty and endurance. Ruth was very subjective to Naomi and before she took any action, she took permission from Naomi and there was nothing she did without the approval of Naomi. At the time when Ruth was gleaning behind the reapers Boaz visited the field and inquired who the woman gleaning the grain behind his reapers was and they told him that she was a Moabite woman who returned with Naomi. Upon hearing that, Boaz encouraged Ruth not to go to any other field but to stay only in his field to glean grain. This was the evidence of another mercy that the Lord has bestowed on Ruth because of her responses to the issues in her family and for her loyalty to Naomi. It was not by chance that Ruth landed in the field of Boaz, but it was through the direction, providence, and the mercy of God. Ruth was surprised and wondered that Boaz was so nice to her. Boaz told her that he had heard of the kindness which Ruth had shown to Naomi and Boaz prayed to the Lord for Ruth. Ruth reported everything which happened to her to Naomi and Naomi was pleased that Ruth ended up in the field of Boaz, a relative. The relationship between Ruth and Naomi grew so strong that Naomi addressed Ruth as daughter instead of as daughter-in-law.

"Now Naomi had a relative of her husband, a man of great wealth, of the family of Elimelech, whose name was Boaz. And Ruth the Moabitess said to Naomi, please let me go to the field and glean among the ears of grain following one in whose eyes I may find favor. And she said to her, Go, my daughter. So, she left and went and gleaned in the field after the reapers; and she happened to come to the portion of the field belonging to Boaz, who was of the family of Elimelech. Now behold, Boaz came from Bethlehem and said to the reapers, May the LORD be with you. And they said to him, May the LORD bless you. Then Boaz said to his servant who was in charge of the reapers, whose young woman is this? And the servant in charge of the reapers replied, she is the young Moabite woman who returned with Naomi from the land of Moab. And she said, 'Please let me glean and gather after the reapers among the sheaves So she came and has remained from the morning until now; she has been sitting in the house for a little while. Then Boaz said to Ruth, Listen carefully, my daughter. Do not go to glean in another field; furthermore, do not go on from this one, but join my young women here. Keep your eyes on the field which they reap and go after them. Indeed, I have ordered the servants not to touch you. When you are thirsty, go to the water jars and drink from what the servants draw. Then she fell on her face, bowing to the ground, and said to him, why have I found favor in your sight that you should take notice of me, since I am a foreigner? Boaz replied to her, all that you have done for your mother-in-law after the death of your husband has been fully reported to me, and how you left your father and your mother and the land of your birth and came to a people that you did not previously know. May the LORD reward your work, and may your wages be full of the LORD, the God of Israel, under whose wings you have come to take refuge Then she said, I have found favor in your sight, my lord, for you have comforted me and indeed have spoken kindly to your servant, though I am not like one of your female servants. And at mealtime Boaz said to her, come here, that you may eat of the bread and dip your piece of bread in the vinegar. So, she sat beside the reapers; and he served her roasted grain, and she ate and was satisfied and had some left. When she got up to glean, Boaz commanded his servants, saying, let her glean even among the sheaves, and do not insult her. Also, you are to purposely slip out for her some grain from the bundles and leave it so that she may glean, and do not rebuke her. So, she gleaned in the field until evening. Then she beat out what she had gleaned, and it was about an ephah of barley. And she picked it up and went into the city, and her mother-in-law saw what she had gleaned. She also took some out and gave Naomi what she had left after she was satisfied. Her mother-in-law then said to her, where did you glean today and where did you work? May he who took notice of you be blessed, so she told her mother-in-law with whom she had worked, and said, the name of the man with whom I worked today is Boaz. Naomi said to her daughter-in-law, may he be blessed of the LORD who has not withdrawn His kindness from the living and from the dead. Again, Naomi said to her, the man is our relative; he is one of our redeemers. Then Ruth the Moabitess said, Furthermore, he said to me, 'You are to stay close to my servants until they have finished all my harvest. And Naomi said to her daughter-in-law Ruth, it is good, my daughter, that you go out with his young women, so that others do not assault you in another field, so she stayed close by the young women of Boaz to glean until the end of the barley harvest and the wheat harvest. And she lived with her mother-in-law" (Ruth 2: 1- 23, NASB).

Naomi was so pleased with Ruth that she wanted Boaz to redeem her for his wife. She set up a scheme to enable Ruth to lie with Boaz. Boaz in response went the normal channel to secure the right to redeem Ruth. After Boaz had secured the right of redemption Ruth became his wife and Ruth had a son through Boaz. The son was named Obed. Obed's son was Jesse, and Jesse was the father of David. (Ruth 3; 13: 21, NASB). It was through the linage of David that Christ the Savior came to this world to save sinners. God rewarded Ruth for her response to the adversities in her life and for her loyalty to Naomi. What a wonderful thing God did to reward Ruth for her great responses. Her responses had a significant impact on all human race through Christ, the Son of God, the Savior.

The Widow and the Prophet

There was drought for a continuous three-year period and there was scarcity of food and water for animals and humans. Prophet Elijah prayed for the drought because of the stubbornness of the people, who with their king refused to follow the guidance of God. But, when the sinful people are suffering the righteous will be affected in a collateral way, as well. Elijah was suffering similar fate as the people. However, God was providing him with supply of food at certain time during the drought. But, it came to a time when God told him to move to another place called Zarephath where God made a provision for him through a widow with a son. The Lord assured Elijah that He had prepared a lady to provide for his needs for food and drink. When Elijah arrived at the place he saw a widow collecting sticks for cooking. Elijah requested the widow to give him water to drink. The widow by her response was going to give Elijah water as he requested. Elijah did not stop with asking for water, but he added to his request. He asked the widow to get him some food to eat, as well. It is commonly said that if 'you give someone a space, the person could take an advantage and drive a truck through.' This was the occasion on the part of Elijah. Although the woman was very hospitable, she was of meagre resource. She did not have a husband to provide for her needs and she had to manage the little she had with her son. The widow had some flour and a small quantity of oil left in the jar. Her intention was for her and her son to share the food that was left and await death. However, she responded positively to Elijah and provided him with the last piece of food meant for her and her son as their last meal together before they die of hunger and thirst. The widow wanted her and her son to eat their last meal and die with full stomachs. But when the request came for an assistance, the widow was not thinking only of the good for herself and her son, but the good and welfare of others. In essence, by giving away the food meant for her and her son she sped up their deaths. As a result of her response in kindness to Elijah, he blessed her, the flour, and the oil. The flour and the oil continually got replenished for her use until the drought subsided. Her response to prophet Elijah gave her the Ife sustaining oil and flour which she and her son needed to be alive during the drought. It was not long before the widow reaped the fruits of her kindness. In a span of time the widow's son got sick and Elijah healed him. (1 King 6:8 - 24, NASB).

Effects of Job's Responses

In this world humans will face difficulties and/or adversities whether one is a follower of God or not. " No temptation has overtaken you except something common to mankind; and God is faithful, so He will not allow you to be tempted beyond what you are able, but with the temptation will provide the way of escape also, so that you will be able to endure it (1 Corinthians 10: 13, NASB). The only difference between Christians and non-Christians is their responses to adversities as to whether they ask for God's help and give Him reference or shun God; blame Him, or run away from Him. God feels human pains and He is constantly working ways to relieve humans from all kinds of adversities, this should serve as comfort to believers of God when going through all kinds of adversities. In the case of Job, he never blamed God, but he gave reference to God. Job's response is a model response for believers of God to emulate. At times it appears that the devil's focus is on those who have their faith in God. In talking to the believers and those around, Paul said, " rejoicing in hope, persevering in tribulation, devoted to prayer" (Romans 12:12). This is the response Jesus expected believers to have when there are tribulations and troubles and when it appears that there is nowhere to turn. Job was a man of good reputation who served God with uprightness and reference. He was blessed with seven sons and three daughters. He was an extraordinarily rich man and he had thousands of camels, hundreds of donkeys, many servants. He was considered the greatest of all the people of the East. Even with all his riches he worshiped God reverently (Job 1: 1 - 5, NASB). God was so proud of Job that He boasted of Job to satan which was the start of Job's tribulations. Then satan challenged God and said that Job was only faithful to God because of the good he had been receiving from God, but if those possessions were to be removed Job would no longer be loyal to God. God was so sure that Job would stay focused on Him regardless of whatever trouble satan brought upon him. In their discussion God put a limit on satan on how much tribulation he could put on Job. The limitation was that he could not kill Job, then God allowed satan to torture Job with all sorts of adversities up to his health. Job lost everything one after the other. Job's tribulations were happening one after the other without a break for him to digest and assimilate one disaster before another occurred. In all his tribulations Job never denied God. In his sufferings Job maintained positive responses to God. He did not blame God for all his problems. "No one is to say when he is tempted, I am being tempted by God, for God cannot be tempted by evil, and He Himself does not tempt anyone" (James 1: 13, NASB).

Reports of adversities began to come in one after the other with the death of his animals, his servants, and eventually the death of his children. When the news of those tragedies came to him, this was how Job responded. "Then Job got up, tore his robe, and shaved his head; then he fell to the ground and worshiped. He said, Naked I came from my mother's womb and naked I shall return there. The LORD gave and the LORD has taken away. Blessed be the name of the LORD. Despite all this, Job did not sin, nor did he blame God" (Job 1: 20 - 22, NASB). In the middle of the tragedy and during his sorrow Job worshiped and blessed God and declared the futility of worldly possessions. When satan realized that despite the loss of his possessions Job did not deny God, he went back to God to get permission to destroy Job's health, but God gave satan a limitation not to kill Job. "Then Satan went out from the presence of the LORD and struck Job with severe boils from the sole of his foot to the top of his head.

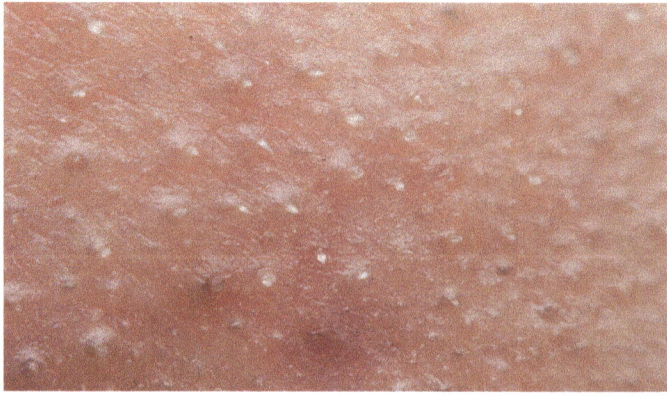

And Job took a piece of pottery to scrape himself while he was sitting in the ashes" (Job 2: 7 - 8, NASB). Job's health condition was so bad and there was no comfortable place for him to lay than in the softness of the ashes.

The itching must have been very severe to the point that he had to use a piece of pottery to scratch himself. Job was in a lot of excruciating suffering and pain with no possibility of getting any relief from his pain by using pain medication since there was no pain medication available for him to take. It must have been exceedingly difficult for him to sleep since his entire body was full of boils and there was no free side to lay. His condition was so deplorable to the point that his wife, due to her love for him, preferred that he died than being in his suffering state. Job's wife was of the knowledge that when people curse God, the instant sure consequence was death. She preferred for Job to be dead than living in continued suffering. As a result of her love for Job she advised Job to curse God and die. His wife was concerned about the condition of his health and about his integrity. She wanted him to die with his integrity intact. However, Job in his response demonstrated his steadfastness to God and despite all his loss and his physical pain he refused to succumb to the wish of satan. He rejected the advice of his wife to curse God and die. He even rebuked his wife for her suggestion to curse God. "Then his wife said to him, "Do you still hold firm to your integrity? Curse God and die! But he said to her, you are speaking as one of the foolish women speaks. Shall we accept good from God but not accept adversity? Despite all this, Job did not sin with his lips" (Job 2: 9 - 10, NASB).

It might have even been easier for him to concentrate on dealing with his issues by himself without the injection of the three so called friends who came and tortured him the more for several days while he was in his emotional and physical pain. They falsely accused him of the sins he never committed and were advising him to confess them. They were 'kicking him when he was down.'

Job's Friends Visited him

"Now when Job's three friends heard about all his adversities that had come upon him, they came, each one from his own place, Eliphaz the Temanite, Bildad the Shuhite, and Zophar the Naamathite; and they made an appointment together to come to sympathize with him and to comfort him. When they looked from a distance and did not recognize him, they raised their voices and wept. And each of them tore his robe, and they threw dust over their heads towards the sky. Then they sat down on the ground with him for seven days and seven nights, with no one speaking a word to him, for they saw that his pain was very great" (Job 2: 11- 13, NASB).

Job Responded in Lamentation for his birth in response to his wife's advice for him to cause God and die, Job cursed and lamented the day of his birth. Job instead of being angry with God was angry with the day he was born and with those who congratulated his mother on the date of his birth.

"Afterward Job opened his mouth and cursed the day of his birth. And Job said, May the day on which I was to be born perish, As well as the night which said, A boy is conceived. May that day be darkness; May God above not care for it, Nor light shine on it. May darkness and black gloom claim it; May a cloud settle on it" (Job 3: 1 - 26, NASB).

Job's Friends' Attitude

Job's three friends visited him and showed some concerns for the condition and sufferings of Job. They were very sympathetic to him initially for seven days and seven nights. They went through the motions of mourning for his condition. But their attitude towards him changed when their egos took over and instead of being continued comforts to him, they were all about their own ego and they turned against him in his sufferings. Instead of comforting him they harassed him with their words and deeds. They did not care about his sufferings, but they were only concerned about elevating themselves. They probably were jealous of Job's riches and how well things were going with Job before his troubles. They pretended to be speaking on behalf of God, but all they were doing was 'kicking Job when he was down.' They felt that they had upper hands on him at his time of trouble without considering how much emotional pain they were inflicting on him in addition to his physical pain. Their focus was how good they looked without considering the effects of their actions on Job's feelings and health conditions. They were taking turns to torture him with their harsh words and lack of sympathy. Job, under the sorrow of the loss of his wealth, children, health, and the torturing of his friends was under uncontrollable painful situation that he requested an audience with God for God to show him what he had done wrong to deserve his sufferings. Job wanted a face-to-face conversation with God to prove his innocence. However, Job thought over his challenge to God and he quickly reversed his challenge to God and stated, "though he slays me, yet will I hope in Him" (Job 13: 15a, NASB). Job's responses were in congruent with the words spoken by Jesus in His pieces of advice to His followers when He said "These things I have spoken to you so that in Me you may have peace. In the world you will have tribulation but take courage; I have overcome the world" (John 16:

33, NASB). Throughout his sufferings Job acted and responded with courage towards God.

When God eventually responded to him, Job realized that he was not worthy to challenge God and he responded with repentance and asked God for forgiveness. God answered job's plea for forgiveness and in return blessed Job. The response of Job to his tragedies resulted in God giving him back all that he had lost. God rewarded Job for his loyalty and steadfastness to Him. "Better to remain silent and be thought a fool than to speak out and remove all doubt" (Abraham Lincoln, Golden Book, Nov. 1931). During the first seven days and seven nights Job might have thought that his friends were true friends to him because they were quiet for all those times and they appeared to be true sympathizers, however, he realized that they were after nurturing their own egos and that they were not true friends to him after they opened their mouths and spoke. At that point all doubts as what kind of friends they were to him varnished. God rebuked Job's three friends for their unkindness to Job by not consoling him and for being harsh to him during his difficulties. Therefore, God humiliated them by asking them to take some animals and sacrifice them before Job and to have Job pray over them. They followed God's instructions and Job prayed over them and they were forgiven.

Response to a Grieving Person

Everybody responds to grief in his/her life in different ways. The way Christians should deal with grief should be remarkably different from the way a non-Christian would respond. However, until a person is hit with grief, only God knows how an individual would respond just as God was sure of how Job was going to respond to the tragedies in his life. Therefore, Christians should pray to God to give them grace in their responses to grief. There was a man who was hit with grief. This man immigrated to another country with his wife.

The relationship between the man and his wife was tenuous. They had three children during their marriage. The wife died in few years after the birth of their last child. The husband was left with caring for the three young children while working a full-time job. The man invited his father from his country of birth to be with him in his adopted country. The father was with him for a while, and they enjoyed each other's company. However, the father died and he took the corpse of his father back to his country of origin for burial. He was full of grief for the death of his father who had been his support and whom he had leaned on for truthful pieces of advice for a while. His children were all grown, and they had graduated from colleges and had obtained employments with different major companies which took them away from him. Although he was lonely living by himself, he got relief, joy, and satisfaction from knowing that his children were all gainfully employed and he was no longer responsible to provide for their needs. He relied on few loyal friends he had and on the members of his Church group. As he was getting recovered from the death of his father news came to him that his daughter who was working in another city collapsed and died at work. With this unexpected terrible event he was devastated and began to question God. He recounted how loyal and how much he worshipped God, prayed to God regularly, and performed good deeds to others, therefore, he felt that God has repaid him evil for his good. He was upset with God and questioned if there is God at all. When Christians approach this man what should be the most Godly way to handle the situation? Is it time to question the man's commitment to God? Is it time to take out the Bible and lecture this man about the word of God and the existence of God? Is it time to insinuate that those hardships happened to him because of his lack of being fully committed to God? Is it time to defend God or use logic to answer the man's many questions and doubts? Is it time to be with the man in quietness? What should the right approach be? In a situation like this it is difficult to know the right approach to take, however, there are some steps one should not take at the moment of his intense grief. A good Christian should not question the man's commitment to God. Just as in the case of Job, all the tragedies in his life were not because of his lack of commitment to God. In fact, it appeared that his tragedies sprang from his commitment to God. Taking out the Bible and reading passages to the man at the time of intense grief might do more harm than good. It might appear as one is questioning the man's faith in God. The man should not be blamed for the hardship he was going through. It might be better and comforting to admit that one does not know the reason those tragedies were happening to him. Such confession might be more helpful to him in his grief than trying to manufacture reasons or accusing the man of any shortcomings because only God knows. It is not time to defend God. God does not need human defense. God can defend Himself and He will do it in due time. Peter tried to defend God (Christ) and his effort was not accepted. Logic could only go so far when dealing with God and things pertaining to God because logic could not answer the misery of God since it is only by faith that one could accept the actions of God because faith in God does not appear logical except for those who have their faith in God and believe Him. Actions of God to humans might not appear to be right or just, but only by asking God for the opening of one's eyes could one see Jesus and understand the misery of God's actions. Therefore, it is important to be subjected to the will of God in dealing with the situation as the man had in order to give him relief from his grief. As Job's friends did during the first seven days and seven nights of visiting him, they were quiet, and Job appreciated

128

their presence and quietness, and it was consoling to him until they started talking that they ruined the value of their presence with him. This should be an example that being present with a grieving person in silence might be better than trying to speak. You should not feel obligated to say something because a quiet presence might speak volumes and more consoling to the person than any spoken words. Endure the uneasiness of staying quiet and resist the self-

imposed pressure that you have to say something to engage the grieving person. Holding a grieving person's hand, or gentle pats on the back, as appropriate, might do better than speaking. In another piece of advice, in a different situation which is based on reliance on God for responses, Jesus said "But when they arrest you and hand you over, do not worry beforehand what to say. Instead, speak whatever you are given at that time, for it will not be you speaking, but the Holy Spirit "(Mark 13: 11; Luke 12: 11; Matthew 10: 19). This piece of advice from Jesus should be encouraging to believers not to worry about what to say in situations requiring a response by relying on the Holy Spirit. In speaking with this man, the Lord will provide the mannerism and the way to speak as directed by the Holy Spirit. Therefore, the only appropriate way to comfort this man is not to go ahead of God, but to allow God to lead the way. With such submission to God's direction, one will surely be a source of comfort to the man and make God real to him. A commitment of praying for the grieving individual could go a long way in giving the individual peace and comfort. Just with your prayers God will surely minister to him. In this world with the existence of the devil tragedies abound, but the name Jesus is greater than the devil.

No Other Name But Jesus
No other Name
When all the storms are raging
In a world where peace cannot be found
And truth is just so hard here
Above the doubts, above the fears
Even in our weakness
There's a grace that will not let us go
A still small voice reminding us
That we are His and that's enough
We cry out from our deep dispair
And find the answer waiting there
No other name
No other name but Jesus
Has the power to heal and set the captive free
No other name
No other name can free us
There's never been a doubt who deserves the glory and the faith
There is no other name
It's written in the pages
Of the stories we've been handed down
It's in the last one who took our place
He calls us to a life of faith
So step by step we follow
With his word let before our feet
Leading us to hear His call
Learn to trust Him through it all
Everything we see in Him
Just reminds us once again
No other name
No other name but Jesus
Has the power to heal and set the captive free
No other name

No other name can free us
There's never been a doubt who deserves the glory and the faith
There is no other name
No other name could raise the dead
Could feed a crowd with some fish and bread
Could whisper peace to calm the sea
Could give his life to ransome me
No other name could raise the dead
Could feed a crowd with some fish and bread
Could whisper peace to calm the sea
Could give his life to ransom me
No other name
No other name but Jesus
Has the power to heal and set the captive free
No other name
No other name can free us
There's never been a doubt who deserves the glory and the faith
There is no other name
Oh, there is no other name

(*The Celebration Hymnal, Songs and Hymns for Worship,*
#15,1997).

With the assurance that the name of Jesus is above all names Christians should be confident to minister to a grieving soul.

Jonah's Response

The Lord wanted to use Jonah for His purpose and for Jonah to be His instrument to save the people of Nineveh. When Isaiah heard the calling from the Lord, his response was of submission and willingness to do the will of the Lord. Isaiah recounted "Then I heard the voice of the Lord, saying, whom shall I send, and who will go for US? And I said, here I am, send me!" (Isaiah 6: 8, NASB). Jonah got similar call, but instead of responding like Isaiah did he responded in rebellion and instead of declaring and submitting himself to the Lord by saying 'here I am, send me,' he decided to run away from the Lord. However, there was one thing Jonah did not realize which was that regardless of wherever he ran, the Lord was there. David declared this truth about the omnipresent nature of God. "Where can I go from Your Spirit? Or where can I flee from Your presence? If I ascend to heaven, You are there; If I make my bed in Sheol, behold, You are there. If I take up the wings of the dawn, If I dwell in the remotest part of the sea, Even there Your hand will lead me, And Your right hand will take hold of me. If I say, Surely the darkness will overwhelm me, And the light around me will be night. Even darkness is not dark to You, And the night is as bright as the day. Darkness and light are alike to You" (Psalm 139: 7 - 12, NASB). The Lord caught up with Jonah on the sea and there was troubled water. A strong wind was tossing their ship around on the sea. The sailors were afraid for their lives, and they started to pray to their gods. When that approach did not work, they decided to throw their belongings into the sea to lighten the ship. But that also did not work and at that time they decided to find the culprit who brought all the impending doom on them. Jonah's sin found him, and he was determined by casting lot to be the culprit. Although the sailors were puzzled and hesitant on what to do to Jonah to calm the sea, they found out that no viable alternative was available to save themselves other than to throw Jonah into the sea. Everywhere Jonah went after

132

disobeying God he was being rejected. At the initial sight of Jonah the sailors willfully accepted him, but once he became the source of their troubles they rejected him and threw him into the sea.

Therefore, the sailors threw Jonah overboard into the sea (Jonah 1: 1- 16, NASB). The sailors lost their belongings, they were afraid for their lives, and they were emotionally traumatized because of the sin of Jonah. This was evident that the sin of one person in a group or in a family could adversely affect the innocent members of the group or the rest of the family. No later than his body hit the sea that a large fish swallowed him (Jonah 1: 17, NASB). The fish joyfully welcomed Jonah into its stomach. The fish was very ecstatic to get a large catch without much effort. The fish might have imagined that Jonah was some sort of food from heaven for it to eat. If the fish could have only imagined that it had swallowed trouble it would not have been so joyous for its catch. The fish got a full stomach and was gleeful that it would not have to work so hard for a while because it has just swallowed a large quantity of protein to be digested gradually for a long time. However, it did not take long before the fish realized that what it had swallowed was trouble. While in the belly of the fish for the three days and three nights he repented and started praying to God for forgiveness. Despite his rebellion to the Lord, the Lord prevented the digestive enzyme in the belly of the fish from digesting Jonah.

It appeared that the Lord inflicted the fish with a stomachache. The fish became nauseated and had a projectile vomiting which threw Jonah out forcefully through its mouth on to a dry land by the seaside (Jonah: 1 – 10, NASB). In other words, the fish stomach evicted Jonah because Jonah's residency in the fish's stomach was a source of trouble for the fish. Until Jonah returned to the Lord, he stood up like a 'sore thumb' and , he was rejected wherever he went or stayed starting with the fishermen in the boat followed by the ejection from the belly of the fish. However, the Lord was with Jonah throughout his rebellion and protected him from any harm when he was living in the belly of the fish for three days and three nights. After three days and three nights of his residency in the belly of the fish and after being vomited on to the shore Jonah responded, reluctantly, to obey the call of the Lord. Jonah went to Nineveh and preached to the people of Nineveh to repent of their sins for God to forgive them and to avoid God's pending destruction. The people of Nineveh repented, and God forgave them (Jonah 3: 1 – 10, NASB). Jonah never learnt that God is more powerful than him, but he remained very obstinate, inwardly. Instead of being happy for what God had done through him, his response was of resentment against God and blaming God for His mercy on the people of Nineveh. Jonah rationalized the reason he did not obey God in the first place and fled to Tarshish. Jonah blamed God for being gracious, compassionate, slow to anger, abounding in love, and relenting from sending calamity on people. Jonah responded irrationally and decided to move away from the congregation of the living. Jonah was so upset that he wished God to take his life for he preferred to die than to live. Jonah isolated himself in a tent expecting the destruction of Nineveh. God teased him by providing him comfort from the heat of the sun through a leafy plant. When Jonah felt amazingly comfortable under the leafy plant God made the leafy plant wither away and Jonah was extremely uncomfortable in the scourging desert heat of the sun. Then Job complained about his discomfort and God pointed out to Jonah that he was upset with the leafy plant which came and went without his contribution. God made clear to Jonah with regards to his response how much more God would respond to the people He created when they repented of their sins. In order words, God was making clear to Jonah that He cared a lot for the people He created. (Jonah 4: 4 - 11, NASB).

Zachariah's Response to the Angel

Zacharias, a priest, was married to Elizabeth. They were both righteous in the sight of God and were doing His will, but they were barren. They were very old beyond the age of bearing children. As Zacharias was performing his priestly service before God in the temple of the Lord burning incense offering an angel of the Lord appeared to him. He was not expecting to see an angel, therefore, he became terribly afraid. However, the angel encouraged him not to be afraid and called him by name to personalize his message to him. The angel told him that God heard his prayers and God had answered them and that Elizabeth would bear him a son to be named John. Zecharias laughed in unbelief because he and his wife were too old to bear a child. Therefore, for his unbelieve his ability to speak was suspended until the child was born. As the priest who oversaw and represented the people before God there was a higher expectation for him to believe the words and messages which came directly from God to him. He had been praying to the Lord fervently, but when God answered his prayers, he doubted God in his response. However, God was very merciful to him because God could have imposed a greater punishment on him for his unbelief, but God only suspended his ability to talk for a little while until the child was born. Have you found yourself praying to God for something without a true believe that God will do it? When God does answer your prayers, are you surprised? If you are surprised, that could be an indication that you did not believe that God would do for you what you have been praying. If that, is you, then confess to God and ask Him to forgive your unbelief? Ask God to make your faith as big as the mustard seed. How much appreciation do you show God for listening to your petition and for doing it according to His will? Zacharias got a little taste of repercussion for doubting God, however, there is no guarantee that your doubting God might result in such a small punishment because it could be bigger. Therefore, it is safe to respond with a trust in God with all of one's heart and not to lean on one's own understanding, but to acknowledge Him in everything. If you find yourself in such position of doubting, confess to God because your punishment might be greater than that of Zacharias'. God answers prayers at His own time and not at the timetable set by humans. However, God might answer in one of three ways, He might tell you to wait, or He might answer it within a period He chooses, but the answer might also not be what you envisage, but better, the Lord might answer by denying your request because He has something better in storage for you. Just remember on those occasions when you must wait, to be patient and if the answer happens to be no, remember that when God closes one door it is because He will open a better door for you. However, be patient and wait for the Lord with thanksgiving in your heart to Him. Remember to, "Rejoice always, pray without ceasing, in everything give thanks; for this is the will of God for you in Christ Jesus" (1 Thessalonians 5: 16 – 18, NASB; Psalm 34: 1, NASB; Ephesians 5: 20, NASB; Philippians 4: 6, NASB; Colossians 3: 17, NASB).

The Shepherds' Response to Joseph and Mary

It would be a good assumption to think that Mary was about nine months pregnant by the time of the census which took them to Bethlehem, a distance of about ninety miles from their home. The Jews were under the rule of the Romans, and they had to do whatever the Roman government demanded without any excuse. It could be a sure bet to say or assume that Joseph and Mary were not rich and could neither afford a quicker nor a more comfortable means of transportation for their journey of about ninety miles. The decree came fast and furious from Caesar Augustus, the emperor and every Roman subject must obey regardless of his/her condition. Regardless of how far along in her pregnancy Mary had no excuse and no choice, but to make a journey of ninety miles from Nazareth in Galilee to Bethlehem in Judea to be counted with Joseph as a family unit of David.

All that Caesar Augustus cared about was to know how many people were under his rule in the Roman empire in order to collect taxes and provide revenue to maintain the fabulous Roman army, to maintain a luxurious Roman Empire, to finance several Roman wars, to build roads, provide amenities, and other infrastructures. In addition to the national census, there were several local censuses in the localities in the Roman Empire the purpose of which was also to collect local taxes (Alyssa Roat). Due to the youthfulness of Joseph and Mary, coupled with the slowness of their journey and meagre resources other people arrived ahead of hem and were able to pay for their rooms in the inn while the rooms were still available. However, when Joseph and Mary arrived in Bethlehem all the rooms in the inn had been taken by those who arrived earlier and had money to rent rooms in the inn. The bigger problem confronting Joseph and Mary was what to do when the time came for the baby to be born. They had to search for a place where the baby could be born with some form of privacy, shelter, and dignity. Since all the rooms in the inn had been taken the only option left was to approach the shepherds for a place to stay. The shepherds must have felt sorry for the young man and his pregnant teenage fiancée. The shepherds responded to the needs of Joseph and Mary and welcomed them into their place even though it might not be an ideal place to have a baby. However, the shepherds were as accommodating as possible (Luke 2: 1- 20, NASB). As a result of their response to Joseph and Mary their names were written indelibly in the plan of God to save the world. They got the visit of angels and they spread the news about the birth of the Savior. What could be the consequence(s) if you respond positively to the call of God for you and for all because He is gently calling for you and for all?

Satan Tempted Jesus

Satan is very clever in determining the need of a person and in his attempt to derail humans. He presents himself as caring and he presents issues in a desirable manner to those he intends to deceive. In his cunning ways he makes his deceits appealing. It is only through the words and power of God that an individual could overcome the power and deceit of satan. This was the approach satan took against Jesus. satan was aware that Jesus was hungry, and it could be easier to do things in order to eat. However, what satan did not realize was that Jesus was not lacking what to eat or could not command food to show up for him to eat, but that he denied Himself food for forty days and forty nights to set Himself apart to do the will of God. Therefore, satan went to Jesus when He was hungry and played on Jesus' ego by saying, "if you are the son of God, command these stones to be turned into bread." Satan by his word was challenging Jesus and implying that if Jesus did not change stones to bread as he had requested Him to do, then Jesus was not the Son of God. If Jesus had listened to satan and did what satan wanted he would have been under the control of satan from that point forward. Jesus would have had to continue to do what satan wanted to satisfy His ego. But, Jesus saw the scheme of the devil for what he was and He responded with the saying "man shall not live on bread alone, but by the word that comes out of the mouth of God" (Matthew 4: 4, NASB). Jesus, with His response to the devil indicated that despite the importance of food, it is not as important as whatever God says and since the devil was not God He was not going to listen to his demands or suggestions. However, the devil persisted in his intention to derail Jesus' missionary plans. The devil wanted Jesus to function as a magician and to receive praise from people by performing stunts. The devil took Jesus to the pinnacle of the temple and challenged him to jump down and if He were truly the Son of God, God would send His angels to protect him. The devil was knowledgeable of the word of God, but he twisted them to satisfy his intentions. The devil is always an expert in playing on people's egos and that was the principle he was using when he was challenging Jesus by saying "if you are the Son of God." However, Jesus was aware of the scheme of the devil, and He told the devil that performing a stunt and expecting God to rescue Him amounted to tempting God. Jesus continued to lecture the devil that God has written that no one should test Him. The devil understood the supremacy of God's words over his, therefore, he did not have any response for Jesus' assertion. The devil was persistent, hoping that Jesus would allow His ego to get the best of Him. But the devil was wrong in his thinking and miscalculated the Lordship of Jesus. As his last act the devil took Jesus to the high mountain to show him all the surrounding kingdoms of the world and their glory. He then told Jesus that if He would subject himself to him and paid him homage and worship him, he (satan) would give all those kingdoms and their glory to Him. The one thing the devil did not realize was that the entire world and its glory belong to Jesus and are under His control. He was attempting to give Jesus what he had already owned. At this point Jesus was done with the devil and He drove him away. The devil came empty handed in his attempt to derail Jesus of His mission. Jesus resisted the devil and the devil eventually fled. (Matthew 4: 5 - 11, NASB). Although the devil was persistent by hanging around Jesus, but Jesus knew that the devil was not a good company for Him, therefore, He commanded the devil to depart from Him. The devil could have probably been hanging around Jesus if He had not commanded him to depart from him. The devil realized the power of who was giving him directives and to prevent bringing trouble on himself the devil departed as fast as the command came out of Jesus' mouth. The devil never returned to badger Jesus henceforth. The Bible is emphatic on how to handle the devil because it is inevitable that the devil would visit everyone, male or female, rich, poor, or in between to tempt him or her. The devil's temptation might be different for individual; however, the intention of the devil is never for human goodness. As a result, the Bible warned in these words, "Be of sober spirit, be on the alert. Your adversary, the devil, prowls around like a roaring lion, seeking someone to devour. So, resist him, firm in your faith, knowing that the same experiences of suffering are being accomplished by your brothers and sisters who are in the world" (1st Peter 5: 8 - 9, NASB). The Bible warns the believers to be on the watchout and to be close to the Lord who could drive away the devil. An adage states that a person cannot prevent a bird from flying over his/her head, but he/she can prevent the bird from making a nest on his/her head. This is the situation with the devil, one cannot prevent the devil from tempting one, but with the help from God one can resist the devil, however, for this to be possible individuals need to move closer to God and away from the devil and his gimmicks.

The Woman of Samaria

The Samaritan woman went to the well to draw water during the heat of the day. Normally in that region because of the scourging heat of the sun women or anyone who wanted to fetch water at the well would go either earlier in the day or later in the evening when the sun might have gone down. However, in the case of this woman she went during the heat of the day. This woman might have gone to the well when no one would go with her and when she would not encounter people at the well. This woman probably was the 'talk' of the city because of her reputation. She had been divorced by five men and she was living with her boyfriend to whom she was not married. It was possible that many people had dissociated themselves from her and she had no friend. Therefore, she went to the well alone to avoid the crowd. In the case of Jesus God directed Him to go through Samaria. There were other routes which Jesus could have taken instead of going through Samaria, but through the divine providence of God to the Samaritan woman Jesus went through Samaria. Another plan of God fulfilled for the Samaritan woman was the fact that she was alone and Jesus was alone because Jesus had sent His disciples to the city to buy them lunch. This situation gave the woman and Jesus ample opportunity to have a candid conversation without the interruptions of others. God set up the stage perfectly well for the woman to talk frankly with Jesus. With God nothing happened/happens by chance or by pure luck, but through His perfect plan everything happened/happens to fulfil His purpose. Jesus encountered the Samaritan woman at the well and requested her to give him water to drink. However, in their culture the Jewish people did not have many things to do with the Samaritans, they lived separated lives and hardly interacted with each other as groups.

The Samaritan woman was aware of that relationship and she responded accordingly. She wondered why Jesus, a Jew, would ask

her for water. In Jesus' response He made clear that He was not just a common Jew and if the Samaritan woman had been aware of who was speaking to her, she would not only have given Him water as requested, but she would have asked for living water from Him. The woman responded in amazement or sarcastically by saying, in essence, are you joking! how are you going to get water out of the well without a bucket or by implication she meant, why are you asking me for water if you could get it for yourself? She continued to indicate that even Jacob, as great as he was, could not even get water from a deep well without a bucket. In her follow up response, she indicated that Jesus was not greater than Jacob who gave them the well. Jesus must have been enjoying the conversation with the Samaritan woman, and He was getting the woman to think deeply about His spoken words. Jesus told her that drinking the water drawn from that well would quench one's thirst temporarily, but the water He had to give would quench her thirst forever and it would become a fountain of water inside the one who has received it and springing up to eternal life. The woman was thinking of how much time and effort it repeatedly took her to go to the well to fetch water and she was imagining how great it would be and how much time she would save by not having to go to the well again to fetch water. The Samaritan woman took the words of Jesus literally and was only thinking of the benefits she could drive from them if they were as Jesus spoke it. Therefore, in her response to Jesus she requested that He give her the water He was talking about. Jesus then requested for her husband to be present. The woman responded in truth by saying that she did not have a husband. Jesus was appreciative of her truthful response and Jesus then told her that she had had five husbands, but the one she was living with was not her husband. At that point the Samaritan woman's eyes were opened and she was convinced that Jesus was a prophet. She was concerned about the tradition of where to worship which was different for the Samaritans and for the Jews. Jesus then made clear to the Samaritan woman that a place of worship was not important, but worshiping the true God is more important. Jesus emphasized that for worship to be acceptable it must be with truth and sincerity of heart because God is a spirit and worshiping God must be with the spirit and in truth. It should not be by pretense or hypocrisy. The Samaritan woman indicated that the Samaritans were ignorant of the right ways to worship God, however she expressed hope in the coming of Christ who would teach them how to truly worship God. Upon hearing the Samaritan woman's response Jesus disclosed Himself to the woman as the Christ who they were expecting. The Samaritan woman got excited and ran back to the city and told all to come and see a man who told her everything about herself. She wondered if the man could be the Christ they have been expecting to come. As a result of the Samaritan woman's testimony the Samaritans in the city came to see Jesus, the Christ. Many Samaritans believed Jesus' words and they were convinced that He was the Savior of the world. Jesus stayed in their city for two days longer before He departed (John 4: 4 - 42, NASB).

Peter's Response to Fear

After Jesus had worked, preached, and performed miracles in the neighboring areas of His hometown He decided to go back home. However, upon getting to His hometown the elite, the people in power, demagogued people against Him and they doubted His knowledge since they knew His family history with no one highly educated in that family, but only expert in carpentry. What happened to Jesus in His hometown visit could be read in the recording by Matthew. "When Jesus had finished these parables, he moved on from there. Coming to his hometown, he began teaching the people in their synagogue, and they were amazed. Where did this man get this wisdom and these miraculous powers?" they asked. Isn't this the carpenter's son? Isn't his mother's name Mary, and aren't his brothers James, Joseph, Simon, and Judas? Aren't all his sisters with us? Where then did this man get all these things? And they took offense at him. But Jesus said to them, A prophet is not without honor except in his own town and in his own home. And he did not do many miracles there because of their lack of faith" (Matthew 13: 53 – 58, NASB). For anyone who has been in a leadership position outside the home, Jesus' declaration of a leader (prophet) not receiving adequate respect in his own home is obvious. Any leader in any position could attest to the fact that those who they lead outside their home listen to them, do what they say, and give them deserved respects than anyone in their own home. Jesus just declared the obvious fact for all to know and not to be surprised or expect anything different. The people in the hometown of Jesus did not welcome Him but doubted His legitimacy. Jesus must have been disappointed at His reception that He decided to withdraw to God, His father. Jesus decided to go to His true home where His father dwells. He withdrew Himself from them to pay attention and have a conversation with God, the only One He could rely on and who He knew would not disappoint Him. Jesus' action is an example for humans to follow whenever disappointment ensures After parents have spent time with their children in the home, they would at times give the kids free time to go out and play on the playground sometimes in the backyard of their homes where they could still monitor them with 'one eye' on the outside of their back yard. Reading the following record by Matthew one will see the example set by Jesus on how and when to take a break from issues to attend to one's physical and spiritual welfare when things are not going as well as one expects. Jesus did not only give Himself a break, but He gave His disciples a break to go and play in the boat out in the other side of the lake while he went to speak with/pray to God. Jesus was concerned about the safety of his disciples by His detractors, therefore He sent them to get off the ground but to get in the boat and go to the other side for their security while they were relaxing. Even at that time Jesus still had his mind on His disciples who were to play in the boat. Jesus was so concerned for their safety in the boat that He sent them to the other side of the lake. Here is Matthew's account:

Immediately, Jesus made the disciples get into the boat and go on ahead of him to the other side, while he dismissed the crowd. After he had dismissed them, he went up on a mountainside by himself to pray. Later that night, he was there alone, and the boat was already a considerable distance from land, buffeted by the waves because the wind was against it. Shortly before dawn Jesus went out to them, walking on the lake. When the disciples saw him walking on the lake, they were terrified. It's a ghost," they said, and cried out in fear. But Jesus immediately said to them: Take courage! It is I. Don't be afraid. Lord, if it's you, Peter replied, tell me to come to you on the water Come, He said. Then Peter got down out of the boat, walked on the water, and came toward Jesus. But when he saw the wind, he was afraid and, beginning to sink, cried out, "Lord, save me!" Immediately Jesus reached out his hand and caught him. You of little faith," he said, why did you doubt? And when they climbed into the boat, the wind died down. Then those who were in the boat worshiped him, saying, truly you are the Son of God" (Matthew 4: 22 – 33, NASB). The disciples must have been aware of Jesus disappointment of what happened to Him in His hometown. They must have realized that he sent them to the other side of the lake for their safety. However, when they saw someone walking on the lake water, they were afraid. However, Jesus realized the reason for their fear and calmed them down by telling them that He was the one and for them not to be afraid. Just as Jesus said in another teaching: "… The gatekeeper opens the gate for him, and the sheep listen to his voice. He calls his own sheep by name and leads them out. When he has brought out all his own, he goes on ahead of them, and his sheep follow him because they know his voice" (John 10: 1 – 4, NASB). When the disciples heard Jesus' voice they recognized it and they calmed down enough for Peter to regain is bravery to join Jesus walking on the water. Peter was ready to go out of the boat and he did because he heard the voice of the true shepherd and he got out of the boat fearless of the lake water. Peter responded positively to the invitation from Jesus, and he walked out of the boat into the lake water without a life jacket because he took Jesus as his life jacket. Therefore, he kept his eyes on Jesus and he floated walking on the water towards Jesus. He was doing well walking towards Jesus on the water with his eyes and all his attention set on Jesus. However, he listened to the sound of the waves, and he looked away and his attention switched to the waves away from Jesus. When Peter had his focus on Jesus he was as light as a feather walking on the raging water, but as soon as Peter responded to his fear by turning his attention away from Jesus and allowed the fear of the waves and the realization that he did not have a life a jacket or a floating device on him he became heavy as a rock and he began sinking. Upon realizing his predicament, he put his eyes back on Jesus who saved him from his peril. The great lesson with this situation is that there is no amount problems swirling around an individual, as long as, the individual keeps his/her eyes on Jesus Christ He will help the individual to overcome. Keep your eyes on the Lord. Louvin Brothers expressed the idea of focusing on Jesus in his song:

> *"Keep your eyes on Jesus*
> *When the tidal waves of trouble 'round you roll*
> *Keep your eyes on Jesus*
> *He will calm the storms of life that cost your soul*
> *Living in a world that's full of sorrow*

We are tried and tempted everyday
Knowing not the secrets of tomorrow
We find rescue when we watch and pray
Keep your eyes on Jesus
When the tidal waves of trouble 'round you roll
Keep your eyes on Jesus
He will calm the storms of life that cost your soul
Keep your eyes on Jesus
When the tidal waves of trouble 'round you roll
Keep your eyes on Jesus."

There are great pieces of advice in the lyrics of the above song for all Christians and for anyone who reads this book to remember and follow.

Jesus' Teaching on Ways to Respond

Jesus started his teaching by referring to the prevailing human attitude at His time, "An eye for an eye and a tooth for a tooth" (Matthew 5: 38, NASB). This prevailing attitude was engrained in the ways people were treating each other. It was like a competition of who could treat the other person worse than he/she was initially treated. There was no room for forgiveness. Jesus' teaching was completely contrary to the prevailing attitude and practices of His time. It was a foreign thought to all who heard Him. However, for all His hearers to know that He was aware of the origin of their practices and attitude He referred them to the prevailing believe. After laying the foundation for His teaching regarding what He knew about their practices He reversed their way of thinking by stressing the relationship which is guarded by love and a renewal of minds. Then He said if someone slaps you on the right face, turn your left, If someone takes your cloth give him your cloak also, if someone forces you to walk one mile walk two, if Your enemy is hungry, feed him.

Pray for those who treat you badly. Bless those who persecute you. Paul echoed the same sentiment when he said, "Bless those who persecute you. Don't curse them; pray that God will bless them" (Romans 12:14, NASB).

In the teaching of Jesus regarding the treatment of someone who has treated the other wrongly He gave the example of a humiliating action of someone slapping the other on the cheek. In the Jewish culture slapping, someone on the cheek is considered one of the most humiliating actions performed on another. It is so repugnant that slapping one on the cheek is punishable by some fines. However, if people are standing in front of each other with the one doing the slapping being righthanded, slapping the right cheek of the other will have to be done by the back of the right hand. In this case slapping someone with the back of the hand is more humiliating than slapping someone with the palm of the hand, therefore, the penalty is double fold. Jesus was addressing the recipient of the unkindly act not to pay back, but to respond in a way that is not humanly natural or easy. Human responses to such unkindly act are to revenge the act by slapping the perpetrator in return. However, Jesus' teaching was emphasizing that human natural responses are not in alignment with Godly responses. But could easily escalate into increased fight, animosity, hatred, chaos, and unhappiness. Someone takes your cloth give him your cloak also, if your enemy is hungry, feed him, pray for those who treat you badly. bless those who persecute you, bless and curse not (Proverbs 25; 21 – 22; Matthew 5: 38 – 48, NASB; Luke 6; 27 - 31; Romans 12:14 - NASB).

Jesus continued his teaching by saying if someone takes your cloth give him your cloak also. How easy is it to respond in the manner Jesus expected and taught? In fact, it is not easy, and it does not give spontaneous gratification which comes with the natural responses. Therefore, for humans the natural way of response gives a quick but less lasting satisfaction and effects.

The Unforgiving Servant

Peter was curious regarding Jesus' teachings about forgiveness, and he wanted to know what limitation could be put on forgiving. His thinking must have been that there needed to the number of times someone should forgive another person. Peter must have been thinking that forgiveness without a limit is untenable because the culprit could be taking advantage of the offended. Peter was used to the old tradition of an eye for an eye. The practice of retaliation was engrained in his brain. However, since he has been with Jesus and has been listening to His teachings about forgiveness, he must have been feeling uneasy about Jesus' doctrine of an endless forgiveness. He decided to hear directly from Jesus what His idea of forgiveness limitation should be. Peter felt that if a number came from Jesus he could hold on to that number and he could go by that number and start keeping a diligent record of offenses and how many times he has forgiven anyone who offended him - the culprit. He probably was thinking that the person would eventually run out of time and grace thus giving him the opportunity to strike back, if that was Peter's intention, he miscalculated how Jesus would respond to him. Peter felt that there should be an end to forgiving someone, but he did not want to follow a doctrine if it did not come from Jesus. Therefore, he asked Jesus, but before Jesus was even able to respond, Peter suggested the number of times to Jesus. "Then Peter came up and said to Him, Lord, how many times shall my brother sin against me, and I still forgive him? Up to seven times?". Jesus responded to Peter instantaneously and said, I do not say to you, up to seven times, but up to seventy-seven times" (Matthew 18: 21 - 22, NASB). Jesus' response to Peter could be seen in another Bible Version, "Jesus saith unto him, I say not unto thee, Until seven times: but, Until seventy times seven" (Matthew 18: 22, KJV). Peter must have been surprised to hear how many times he needed to forgive. He must have considered that it was better to forgive and forget than to take on another responsibility of counting how many times one has been offended and how many times one has forgiven the offender. The question by Peter gave Jesus a prime opportunity to dwell more on the importance of forgiving others as God has forgiven and made provision for all to receive His forgiveness. Since God took the first step in forgiving humans Jesus emphasized the importance of humans forgiving others to continue to receive God's forgiveness. To bring the point home Jesus told the parable of the unforgiving servant. "For this reason, the kingdom of heaven is like a king who wanted to settle accounts with his slaves. And when he had begun to settle them, one who owed him ten thousand talents was brought to him. But since he did not have the means to repay, his master commanded that he be sold, along with his wife and children and all that he had, and repayment be made. So, the slave fell to the ground and prostrated himself before him, saying, 'Have patience with me and I will repay you everything. 'And the master of that slave felt compassion, and he released him and forgave him the debt" (Matthew 18: 23 - 27, NASB). The widespread practice at the time was to sell a debtor who is not able to pay his debt into slavery and get as much money as the creditor could get out of the sale to repay a portion, if not all the debt, with the believe that getting back some amount of the debt is better than getting nothing. Not only the debtor was sold but the members of the debtor's family were sold, as well. The master of the servants must be closing his books, probably at the end of the year and his accountant gave him the record of his debtors. One of the debtors owed him a lot of money. The servant owed his master ten thousand talents. 1 talent weighs about 33 kilograms (kg). 1 kilogram is equivalent to 1000 grams; therefore, 33 kilograms is equal to (1000 x 33 grams) 33,000 grams. 1 gram of talent is worth $38.00. The total worth of 1 talent is ($38.00 X 33,000) = $1,254,000.00. The master forgave his servant 10,000 talents which is equal to (10,000 x $1,254,000.00) $12,540,000,000,00. Therefore, the servant owed his master $1,254,000) X (10,000) = $12,540,000,000.00.

The servant was fully aware that he could not pay the debt even if all the members of his household were sold including his personal belongings all would not be close to paying a fraction of his debt.

The only last thing he could do was to beg for mercy. It was a lot of money for the master to let go. Regardless of the loss to the master he forgave the servant. "But the one who did not know and did what deserved punishment will receive a light beating. From everyone who has been given much, much will be required; and from the one who has been entrusted with much, even more will be expected" (Luke 12: 48, CSV). It was a lot of money which the master forgave his servant and based on Luke 12: 48 he was expected to reciprocate similar kindness and forgiveness to whoever owed him anything. It became a common knowledge to the rest of the servants in the organization how generous their master was in forgiving the debt of one of them. The news of it must have gone throughout the organization like a wildfire in the forest. How did the forgiven servant respond to the kindness afforded him by his master? "But that slave went out and found one of his fellow slaves who owed him a hundred denarii; and he seized him and began to choke him, saying, 'Pay back what you owe! So, his fellow slave fell to the ground and began to plead with him, saying, Have patience with me and I will repay you. But he was unwilling, and went and threw him in prison until he would pay back what was owed" (Matthew 18: 28 - 30, NASB). The response of the servant who his master forgave a lot of his debt was cruel to another servant who owed him an infinitesimal (extremely small) amount of money. His fellow servant begged him and promised to pay him back but instead of showing kindness to him he choked him and demanded that he pay him right away.

He had his debtor, his fellow servant who was even not a stranger to him, but a co-worker for the same master who forgave him his own debt. His debtor begged him and promised to pay him all that he owed him, but he did forgive him. Instead of showing mercy, he had him arrested, convicted, and put in jail for a very insignificant amount of money owed. The master of the unforgiving servant forgave him $12,540,000,000.00 but he did not forgive a fellow servant who owed him the equivalent of $207.3, (1 denarius on December 7, 2021, was $2.073).Therefore, 100 denarii equal to (100) X ($2.073) = $207.3), but he had him put into jail. However, just as the news of the forgiveness of his debt by their master went around the organization so was the news of his treatment of his fellow servant travelled around the organization. All the servants marveled at his behavior and the treatment of a co-worker. "So when his fellow slaves saw what had happened, they were deeply grieved and came and reported to their master all that had happened. Then summoning him, his master said to him, 'You wicked slave, I forgave you all that debt because you pleaded with me. Should you not also have had mercy on your fellow slave, in the same way that I had mercy on you?' And his master, moved with anger, handed him over to the torturers until he would repay all that was owed him. My heavenly Father will also do the same to you, if each of you does not forgive his brother from your heart. (Matthew 18: 31 - 35, NASB). By the time Jesus finished His discourse Peter and all Jesus' disciples and hearers must have gotten a clear picture that there was no need for counting offenses and forgiveness if a person's heart is right with true forgiveness. Jesus equated the master to God, the master reversed his decision of forgiving the ungrateful, unforgiving servant of his decision to forgive a gigantic amount the servant owed him. In this parable Jesus emphasized that forgiveness should come from the heart to be acceptable to God. God who is able to read everyone's heart does not accept a fake forgiveness which does not come from the heart. Forgiveness in which one does not forget but continues to count incidents of offenses and holding grudges are not genuine and as a result God does not accept it. For God to forgive the sins of all human beings they must forgive those who sin against them sincerely. Just as the unforgiving servant owed so much to his master which he did not have the capacity to pay so are human beings so indebted to God that they will never be able to pay back God by their credit/merit, but God paid it all through the shedding of the spotless blood of Christ. In order for everyone to be equal before God and to enjoy similar provision and forgiveness Christ died for the sinful. Jesus paid it all.

I hear the Savior say,
"Thy strength indeed is small;
Child of weakness, watch and pray,
Find in Me thine all in all."
Refrain:
Jesus paid it all,
All to Him I owe;
Sin had left a crimson stain,
He washed it white as snow.
For nothing good have I
Whereby Thy grace to claim;
I'll wash my garments white
In the blood of Calv'ry's Lamb.
And now complete in Him,
My robe, His righteousness,
Close sheltered 'neath His side,
I am divinely blest. Lord, now indeed I find
Thy pow'r, and Thine alone,
Can change the leper's spots leopard's
And melt the heart of stone.
When from my dying bed
My ransomed soul shall rise,
"Jesus died my soul to save,"
Shall rend the vaulted skies.
And when before the throne
I stand in Him complete,
I'll lay my trophies down,
All down at Jesus' feet.
(The Celebrational Hymnal, Songs and Hymns for Worship, #305).

"You see, at just the right time, when we were still powerless, Christ died for the ungodly. Very rarely will anyone die for a righteous person, though for a good person someone might possibly dare to die. But God demonstrates his own love for us in this: While we were still sinners, Christ died for us" (Romans 5: 6 - 8, NIV). Jesus refinanced human beings' sins, put it on His account, and paid it all with his blood. "For the wages of sin is death, but the gracious gift of God is eternal life in Christ Jesus our Lord" (Romans 6: 23, NASB). If someone should ask you to judge the unforgiving servant, what will your judgement be considering how much he was forgiven and how he treated another servant, a coworker, who owed him a minuscule amount compared to how much his master forgave him? If you will be truthful, you would judge him harshly. Based on the assumption of your judgement, imagine the Lord forgives you not one time, but every time. The Lord forgives you not once but every time that you confess to Him of your sins and ask Him for forgiveness. With that being the case examine how forgivable you are of others who sin against you. Consider your treatment of the drivers on the road with you. If the driver cuts you off, invades your lane, what is your response? Do you curse and yell, or project any unwelcoming gesture to the driver who has invaded your lane? Or do you excuse the action of the driver? Do you consider that there might be something unpleasant happening in the life of the driver and that he/she might be driving on the road, but his or her mind might be preoccupied with the unpleasant event in his/her life? How pleasant will your day be if your response is of consideration and patience for such driver. What effect could your action be on the feelings of such driver, although you might not get immediate gratification of being inconsiderate, but the Lord will bless you for your response. If you are in a store and it happens that the one behind you has fewer items than you have which means that it will take longer time for you to get through the checker and pay than the one behind you who has fewer items to complete and pay, do you give up your place for him/her to go ahead of you? If you allow him/her to go ahead of you, a feeling of peace might fall on you and you might feel good about your action and the Lord will bless you for your act of kindness. Such act of kindness considers the wellbeing of others' first. Paul admonished believers in the way to treat others in this statement, "Do nothing from selfishness or empty conceit, but with humility consider one another as more important than yourselves. "(Philippians 2: 3, NASB). These are the model of responses God expects of those who are called by His name.

Invitation to the Webring Feast

Israel

Wedding celebration is a joyous occasion as a new family is being formed. The parents of the bride and the groom invite their friends, family members, and acquaintances to celebrate the occasion with them. Rich people or those in the leadership positions such as kings and politicians make it an elaborate occasion. The hosts generally wanted every aspect of the wedding organized including the garments worn by the guests. In ancient tradition kings provided garments for their guests. This practice was evident when Pharaoh provided garments for Joseph's brothers before they went to see him (Genesis 45: 22; Relmar Schutze). For the guests to be presentable and uniform in appearance the host bought garments for the guests. As they arrived at the site of the wedding ceremony before going inside, they were to shed their clothes and change into the garment provided by the host. In this occasion the invited guests disappointed the host by disregarding the invitation at the last moment. When guests were not showing up the host (the king) sent reminders to the guests to alert them that the wedding ceremony was about to start and for them to hurry and attend. The king did not send only one servant as reminders but several, however the responses of the invited guests were dismal and disappointing. As the time for the wedding ceremony was running out, the king was so disappointed at

160

his invited guests for whom he had provided food and drink to enjoy. He then sent out his servants to just go outside into the neighborhood and invite whoever they were able to find. The servants were able to get some impromptu guests to respond positively to attend the wedding feast. As the impromptu guests arrived, they took the wedding garments provided for them, but one impromptu quest decided not to wear the wedding garment provided which was an insult to the host. The rest of the impromptu guests were very diligent in wearing the wedding garment before going in. The one of the impromptu guests did not care, not that the garment would cost him any money to wear and not that there were not enough garments for every guest, but he responded with an uncaring attitude. This impromptu guest acted as a party crasher. When the king went out to see the wedding guest and to thank them for their acceptance of his last-minute invitation he spotted a man who was not wearing the wedding garment which he provided for all to wear . The king was infuriated and commanded that he be bound and thrown out into the darkness. The responses of the original invitees were insulting and uncaring to the king and the effects of their responses on the whole wedding ceremony. The impromptu guests enjoyed the food and the fellowship with other invitees. The one impromptu guest who refused to wear the wedding garment provided met the wrath of the king because of his response. After being disappointed by the original invitees the king was in no mood to tolerate any other detractor. (Matthew 22: 1- 14, NASB). God as the King has invited you to a wedding feast, He had provided you the sacrificial lamb and had sacrificed Him on the altar of the cross and He is inviting you. Will you reject Him to the end? If you agree and go to His wedding ceremony, will you accept the salvation He has provided, or will you reject it? The only qualification required for you to be accepted into His wedding feast is to put on the garment He has already provided for you which is the acceptance of Christ as your Savior and Lord. That requirement is free for all with no cost attached so you could party with God. Will you be in God's wedding feast, Christ has paid the cost? Will you party with Him and His Son? Jesus said, "Behold, I stand at the door and knock; if anyone hears My voice and opens the door, I will come into him and will dine with him, and he with Me" (Revelation 3:20, NASB).

Will you open the door of your heart to Him? He is patiently waiting, waiting for you and for me.

"Softly and tenderly
Jesus is calling
Calling for you and for me
See on the portal
He's watching and waiting
Waitin' for you and for me
Come home
Come ho-ome
He who are wary
Come ho-ome
Ernestly, tenderly
Jesus is calling
Calling, oh sinner
Come home
Come home
Come ho-ome
He who are wary
Come ho-o-ome
Ernestly, tenderly
Jesus is calling
Calling, oh sinner
Come home
(Will L. Thompson; The Celebration Hymnal Songs and Hymns
for Worship, #479)

Response of the Ten Virgins

In His discussion about being prepared for the kingdom of God Jesus emphasized the importance of getting it done when there is still daylight to see what one is doing in order to be able to do it well. Since the daylight time is limited in most parts of the world and majority of His hearers were farmers, He used the analogy of farmers working hard during the daylight hours. Once night fell farmers were not able to work in darkness. Therefore, no time should be wasted when there is still opportunity to work or to serve God when it comes to the spiritual matters. Jesús continued similar sentiment regarding the kingdom of God with the parable of the ten virgins. The ten virgins were members of a marriage ceremony which was to take place at night. All the ten virgins were aware that the marriage would take place at night and that it was going to be dark. They must have been instructed that the light in the wedding hall would be turned off and other guests at the wedding would be sitting in darkness, but the virgins were to light the ways for the groom as they lead him to the stage. This practice would undoubtedly direct the attention of the attendees to the entourage of the groom. This was a spectacular scene envisioned by the host of the wedding. For this to work as well as envisioned all the ten virgins must be ready at the last-minute call to go in with the groom. It meant that they must be well prepared with all the supplies with them to be ready to go in with the groom. Since the marriage might take a long time for the ceremony to be completed, they must have adequate supply of all that they would need to last the duration of the wedding at night. Every virgin was to be prepared to have a lamp to light her way during the marriage procession. It was a honor to be invited to participate in the procession of such a marriage ceremony. This was a lifetime opportunity which many people would take very seriously and arrive at the ceremony promptly without delay and be well prepared. In order for everything to fall into place without disappointing the host many people would take time to prepare, look over all items on their list that they would need for the night of the wedding ceremony and not wait until the last minute. Most people would take their responsibility very seriously in order not to disappoint the groom. They would look over their list several times ahead of the day and on the day of the ceremony to be sure that nothing was overlooked or forgotten. They would not relax or rest until they were sure that they were fully ready to meet the groom within a minute's notice. Five of the ten virgins prepared well, five of them did not prepare well and took everything for granted. They were so comfortable in their lack of preparation and readiness that they went to sleep. They were in their deep sleep when the announcement was made to go and meet the groom and accompany him to the wedding site. All that the five (five wise virgins) who were well prepared had to do was to get up from their sleep, get the light from their lamps going, and were ready to accompany the groom. In their preparation they had extra oil for their lamps so they could maintain their lights functioning throughout the lengthy wedding ceremony. They were sure that the extra oil would be enough for the length of the marriage ceremony but did not have any oil to spare. The other five unprepared virgins (foolish virgins) were awakened from their sleep, but they were not ready to go in with the groom because they did not have their lamps ready to provide the light needed to accompany the groom. As a last ditch effort, they pleaded with the five prudent virgins to give them some oil for their lamps. It was the wrong time for the foolish virgins to be seeking solution to their problems. There is a saying which was appropriate for the situation, the saying goes like this 'your lack of preparation is not my emergency' The five wise virgins declined to assist the five foolish virgins for lack of time to do so and for the fear that giving them oil for their lamps might deplete their supply of oil. Therefore, the five wise virgins advised the foolish virgins to go out and buy their own oil, something they should have done ahead of time. Upon arrival of the groom the five prudent virgins went in with the groom to honor him. As soon as everyone entered the wedding arena, the marriage ceremony began, and the doors were locked to prevent stranglers from interrupting the program of the marriage. When the foolish virgins arrived from pursuing oil for their lamps the marriage ceremony had commenced, and they were no longer allowed to enter the venue. They were locked outside where they were full of all kinds of sorrow and retrospection which no longer counted. (Matthew 25: 1 - 13, NASB).

The warning in this parable for humankind is that God has invited all, and it is only by entering with the groom through the door that the opportunity to attend His marriage feast is available. What are your responses or what will your response be when there is still time? Jesus is calling for all to come to Him because He is the way and the truth and no one can go to the Father, but only through Him. "Jesus said to him, I am the way, and the truth, and the life; no one comes he Father except through Me" (John 14: 6, NASB). In order to get to God, you must enter with the Groom – Jesus Christ – the Way and the Truth.

The Rich man and the Kingdom of God

Just then a man came up to Jesus and asked, "Teacher, what good thing must I do to get eternal life? Why do you ask me about what is good? Jesus replied. There is only One who is good. If you want to enter life, keep the commandments. Which ones? he inquired. Jesus replied, You shall not murder, you shall not commit adultery, you shall not steal, you shall not give false testimony, honor your father and mother, and love your neighbor as yourself. All these I have kept, the young man said. What do I still lack? Jesus answered, If you want to be perfect, go, sell your possessions and give to the poor, and you will have treasure in heaven. Then come, follow me. When the young man heard this, he went away sad, because he had great wealth. Then Jesus said to his disciples, Truly I tell you, it is hard for someone who is rich to enter the kingdom of heaven.

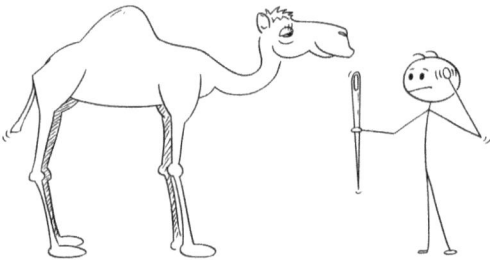

Again I tell you; it is easier for a camel to go through the eye of a needle than for someone who is rich to enter the kingdom of God." (Luke 19; 16 – 24, NIV; NKJV). The rich young man went to Jesus being proud of his achievement in observing the laws. He felt that there should not be anything left to impede him from entering the Kingdom of God. The young rich man felt entitled to entering the Kingdom of God because of his deeds and not because of his believe and reliance in/on God. He thought that he had done every imaginable thing for him to earn the Kingdom of God. However, he was very disappointed when Jesus told him that there was one last obstacle in his way to enter the Kingdom of God. The only obstacle in his way was his riches on which he relied instead of relying on God. Jesus' piece of advice for the rich man was to get rid of the stumbling block in his way. The rich man who felt secure in all that was needed to enter the Kingdom of God was very disappointed to hear Jesus telling him to sell all his riches and help the poor. He probably had looked down on those poor individuals with the thought that they were all lazy people looking for handouts. For Jesus to tell him to go and sell his hard-earned wealth and to assist the poor whom he considered to be lazy people was not anything he was willing to do even if it meant losing the Kingdom of God. He chose to lose the Kingdom of God rather than selling his possessions and help the poor. He was so angry that he steamed away from the presence of Jesus. His response put him in a potential position for the loss of the Kingdom of God.(Matthew 25: 1 - 10, NASB).

Jesus considered the impossible to be possible than for those who rely on their riches instead of relying on God to enter the Kingdom of God. The rich man did not give God a chance to see what God would do if he had listened and followed the directives from Christ. The rich man was not patient in his response to test and see what God would do. The Bible said, "Bring the whole tithe into the storehouse, so that there may be food in My house, and put Me to the test now in this, says the LORD of armies, if I do not open for you the windows of heaven and pour out for you a blessing until it overflows" (Malachi 3: 10, NIV). With rash response by the rich man he did not wait, he was not patient to see how God would fulfil His promise to reward those who have given to His Kingdom on earth materially and how God could reward him with the inheritance of His Kingdom which he was seeking. His response forfeited everything for him. The rich man was blinded by his riches and the thought of losing them to support the poor infuriated him to the point that he did not care any longer about inheriting the Kingdom of God. Therefore, he went away empty handed.

Response of The Rich Fool

Then he said to them, "Watch out! Be on your guard against all kinds of greed; life does not consist in an abundance of possessions. And he told them this parable: The ground of a certain rich man yielded an abundant harvest. He thought to himself, 'What shall I do? I have no place to store my crops. Then he said, This is what I'll do. I will tear down my barns and build bigger ones, and there I will store my surplus grain. And I'll say to myself, You have plenty of grain laid up for many years. Take life easy; eat, drink and be merry. But God said to him, 'You fool! This very night your life will be demanded from you. Then who will get what you have prepared for yourself?' This is how it will be with whoever stores up things for themselves but is not rich toward God." (Luke 12: 15 – 21, NIV). With the above parable Jesus pointed out that the greediness of humans does not do any good towards inheriting the Kingdom of God. Whatever achievement a person acquires the glory should always be ascribed to God who is the giver of all good things. In this parable God blessed the farmer, but instead of thinking of how he could be of service to God and to other human beings from his harvest his focus was directed only towards himself. He was thinking of how he could be living in pleasure for the rest of his life without creating room for God in his plan. He believed that the achievements with his farm product was because of his goodness without giving praise to God of all goodness. Whatever achievement a human being got/gets should provide an opportunity to praise God and to serve others. The rich fool forgot or did not understand this principle and for his response he lost his life. James was emphatic in saying that human beings should involve God in their activities before embarking on it. This is because only God is in control of every person's life and humans should not behave and respond as if he/she is in total control, therefore, in whatever a person is planning to do, God should be invited to participate. The rich fool's response was without involving God and that resulted in his premature death. "Come now, you who say, Today or tomorrow we will go to such and such a city and spend a year there and engage in business and make a profit. Yet you do not know what your life will be like tomorrow. You are just a vapor that appears for a little while and then vanishes away. Instead, you ought to say, "If the Lord wills, we will live and also do this or that" (James 4:13-15 NASB). The statements and parables above emphasize reliance on God and the willingness to follow God's leads in whatever a person does or plans to do. How reliant are you on God? Consider how much if you invite God into your plans, the consequences could favorably surprise you if you give place to God in your life and in the management of your possessions and achievements.

The Ten Talents

A Rich man was ready to go on an extended vacation away from his business which provided him stead income. During his time away he still wanted his business to be productively functional and bringing in money. He had servants who had been working for him, most likely, for a while. He has watched their performances and knew their abilities and how much responsibility each could manage. Based on his knowledge of their abilities he decided to apportion his wealth to each in order to continue to earn revenue from his wealth. He gave out eight talents in total ($1,254,000 X 8 = $10,032,000.00) to his servants, to one he gave five talents ($1,254,000.00 X 5 = $6,270,000.00) to another he gave two talents ($1,254,000.00 X 2 = $2, 508, 000.00), and to the third he gave one talent ($1,254,000.00). His decision was based on his knowledge of the abilities of the three. In an organization such as this man had there must have been many servants, but he trusted those three servants to be able to handle his wealth the best. Therefore he put his trust in them, however, not blindly, but according to the ability of each. He entrusted so much of his wealth to them and went on his long vacation. Two of the servants were very jubilant that their master considered them worthy of his trust that he gave certain portion of his wealth to them to manage while he was away. They were very enthusiastic and did not want to disappoint their master when he returned. Therefore, they went to work right away with the investment their master entrusted to them. They worked so hard that each of them doubled the amount given him by their master. The servant who received one talent was selfish, lazy, jealous, and was terribly upset comparing what he received to what others received without considering his own ability. By his action he proved the master right in his decision to give him only one talent. The master must have been thinking on minimizing his potential loss and that might be the reason he gave him only one talent in the first place. The one servant who received one talent decided not to do anything with what he got, but instead buried it in the ground. He just rendered his master's investment non-productive in the ground where he buried it. The day of accounting came when the master returned, and every recipient of his wealth had to give account of what he had done with them. The one who received five talents had his head raised high and proceeded with joy in his heart to proudly report to his master that he had increased the investment given to him a hundred percent. His master was so happy with him, praised him, and blessed him. The one who received two talents was very happy with himself because of his hard work which made it possible for him to double the amount invested through him by his master. He proudly reported his achievements to their master who rewarded him with high praise and blessings. When he came to the third servant, he was full of rage, he was angry, and upset with his master. Instead of looking at his role in the perception his master had of him to have given him only one talent he accused the master by projecting his own shortcomings on his master. He refused to take responsibility for his own actions. His master was terribly disappointed and upset with him in return and terminated him from his position in the organization. He threw him out of his presence and the servant lost everything. The servant was out of the master's horizon because of his attitude He should have been grateful and appreciative that his master ever remembered to give him any talent at all. If he had been grateful and handled his master's investment well, he could have gotten a bigger investment in the future, but his feelings of self-importance destroyed everything for him. (Matthew 25: 14 - 30, NASB).

There are some lessons to learn from this parable. God gives to each person according to individual's ability. "We have different gifts, according to the grace given to each of us. If your gift is prophesying, then prophesy in accordance with your faith; if it is serving, then serve; if it is teaching, then teach; if it is to encourage, then give encouragement; if it is giving, then give generously; if it is to lead, do it diligently; if it is to show mercy, do it cheerfully" (Romans 12: 6 - 8, NIV). God has never asked a person to do anything for which he/she was not equipped, but all God expects is a willing heart to follow His directions based on the talents which He has given each. God is always ready to give directions and assistance as needed if one yields to His directions and not bury the talent(s) received from God. He has given some talents to each even though they are not always the same. God knows the ability of individuals and He expects everyone to use the talents he or she has received to his or her potential.

Arrest of Jesus

"While He was still speaking, behold, a crowd came, and the one called Judas, one of the twelve, was preceding them; and he approached Jesus to kiss Him. But Jesus said to him, Judas, are you betraying the Son of Man with a kiss? However, Judas did not respond, in fact, Judas might have been surprised of how Jesus knew the intent in his heart before he did anything. When those who were around Him saw what was going to happen, they said, Lord, shall we strike with the sword? And one of them struck the slave of the high priest and cut off his right ear. But Jesus answered and said, Stop! No more of this. And He touched his ear and healed him." (Luke 22: 47 - 50, NASB).

Peter Cut the Servants Ear Off

'And He withdrew from them about a stone's throw, and He knelt down and began to pray, saying, Father, if You are willing, remove this cup from Me; yet not My will, but Yours be done. Now an angel from heaven appeared to Him, strengthening Him" (Luke 22: 41 - 43, NASB). There was a time when Jesus' humanity came through when as His customary practice He went to pray alone. The time for the fulfilment of the reason He came to the world as human was coming to fruition. He was beginning to envisage the weight of the torture and the agony of the sins of the world that was about to fall on Him. In His humanity He wanted to avoid what was ahead of Him, however, as that thought came to His mind the Spirit of God in Him reminded Him of His agreement with God and He immediately recounted and submitted Himself back to the will of the Father. He deferred to the Father for what was best to accomplish God's purpose for humanity. As human, Jesus became weak, however, God did not abandon Him in His humanity, but God sent an angel from heaven to give Him strength. With the renewed strength Jesus was ready to carry the sins of the world and face human consequences for it to save the world from eternal condemnation if they accept Him as their personal Savior, who He is. There was nothing to stop Him any longer from carrying out His mission. While Jesus was being arrested Peter 'rolled up his sleeves' and was ready for a fight. He took the sword and cut off a slave servant's right ear. Jesus, in His renewed strength did not tolerate Peter's action and He sternly commanded him or anyone else with similar intention to stop. Jesus made clear to them in the following statements that He was not powerless and that those arresting Him were mere men with no power that could match His own. He only subjected Himself to the treatment He was receiving to save sinners. "And behold, one of those who were with Jesus reached and drew his sword, and struck the slave of the high priest and cut off his ear. Then Jesus said to him, put your sword back into its place; for all those who take up the sword will perish by the sword. Or do you think that I cannot appeal to My Father, and He will at once put at My disposal more than twelve legions of angels? When Jesus was talking about legions of angels, He meant a large number of angels. In the Roman army a legion comprised of 6,000 elite soldiers. Therefore, the number of angels Jesus told His disciples that He could ask God to provide was

more than twelve legions. By the Roman calculation, the number of angels will be more than seventy-two thousand angels (6,000 X 12 = 72,000), however Jesus said more than 12 legions. Therefore, the numbers of Angels was not determinative, but the number was more than seventy-two thousand (>72,000), (Tony Mariot) https://qr.ae/TWrUui However, with such resources available to Him, Jesus submitted Himself to be tutored by mere human beings to save all.

How then would the Scriptures be fulfilled, which say that it must happen this way?" (Matthew 26: 51 - 54, NASB). The action of Peter was not congruent with the teachings of Jesus throughout His ministry regarding retaliation. Jesus' teachings pointed to revenge as the work of the devil, and he had discouraged everyone who had listened to Him to refrain from the act of revenge in any form. In some of Jesus' discourses He said if your enemy is hungry feed him or her ,if he or she is thirsty give him or her something to drink. Jesus even went further to command or encourage His followers or hearers to pray for their enemies and those who have treated them badly. In an attempt to impress upon His hearers on the importance of forgiving or reconciling with those who (their enemies) had done wrong to them. He said that if they were about to present their offering on the altar but remembered those who had offended them and against whom they were still holding grudges that they should stop, put down their gifts and go and reconcile with those who had offended them before returning to complete giving their offering. "Therefore, if you are presenting your offering at the altar, and there you remember that your brother has something against you, leave your offering there before the altar and go; first be reconciled to your brother, and then come and present your offering (Matthew 5: 23 - 24, NASB).

What Jesus was saying was that even if you are not the one who made enemy with someone else, but if it is someone else who made you an enemy if you are aware of it, it then becomes your responsibility to work on reconciling with the individual. Until you have accomplished that goal or that you have done your best to reconcile with the individual you should not continue to do things as usual. You should find a way to reconcile with him/her if you are aware of it. On another occasion Jesus reminded His followers that if they did not forgive those considered as their enemies their sins, their Heavenly Father would not forgive them too. Jesus saw the action of Peter as a form of revenge and retaliation against those who considered Jesus their enemy and who were trying to arrest Jesus. The action of Peter appeared to be a noble course; however, it was against the teachings of Jesus about forgiveness, reconciliation, or no retaliation. If Jesus had allowed such actions to go unchecked, it would have negated His teachings and it would have been against the purpose for which Jesus came to the world - to save sinners from the perils of their sins. If Jesus had allowed Peter's action to go on unchecked, Jesus' teachings would have had no effect because He would have been considered a hypocrite. The manner in which Jesus' followers and disciples behaved had a reflection on Jesus, therefore, if Jesus had allowed Peter's action to stand it would have had a negative impact on Jesus' message and purpose from that point onward. The action of a leader in the secular environment dictates to the followers and the subordinates how they should behave. If a leader, Chief Executive Officer, an administrator, a manager, or any leader in position of authority treats people, clients, customers, or acquaintances harshly the followers might believe it to be the right way to treat others. Therefore, Jesus did not want to leave the impression that the retaliative action of Peter was acceptable, as a result He stopped Peter quickly in his track. There is a saying about a 'proverbial crow. 'The 'proverbial crow' is tough to eat and does not taste good, therefore, it is important to eat a 'proverbial crow' quickly when it is warm because when it is cold and simmer it is not easy to eat, it is very tough, and tastes worse. The 'proverbial crow' is an analogy for an unpleasant situation/issue. When there is an unpleasant situation the earlier it is managed and resolved the better it is, however, the longer the unpleasant situation is allowed to linger, fester, and simmer without resolution the worse the situation becomes. Jesus did not want the impression of Peter's action to linger and fester, therefore, He stopped it right away. Jesus did not only stop it, but He corrected the wrong done by Peter immediately. Jesus restored the ear of the slave servant.

Jesus Response at His Crucifixion

Jesus suffered mistreatments, beatings, being spit on, false accusations by false witnesses and verbal harassment by the officials. Through all those sufferings He did not resist but submitted Himself to the terrible treatments which He received in order to save sinners from eternal condemnation.

"And when they came to the place called The Skull, there they crucified Him and the criminals, one on the right and the other on the left. But Jesus was saying, Father, forgive them; for they do not know what they are doing." (Luke 23; 33 - 34, NASB). Despite all the bad treatments, lies, insults, punishments, and hatred hauled at Him Jesus responded kindly to them. Jesus felt that they were ignorant. Jesus gave them the benefit of the doubt and He prayed for them. For all the terrible treatments He had received and was yet to receive Jesus considered them ignorant and He prayed to God, the Father, to forgive them. Earlier before this time Jesus taught about refraining from revenge and He urged His followers and his hearers to forgive their enemies and to pray for those who treated/treats them badly. "…But I say to you, love your enemies and pray for those who persecute you," (Matthew 5: 43 - 48). When Jesus was face to face with the difficulties of His life, He lived up to His teachings, realizing the purpose for His sufferings.

"However, it was our sicknesses that He Himself bore,
And our pains that He carried;
Yet we ourselves assumed that He had been afflicted,
Struck down by God, and humiliated.
But He was pierced for our offenses,
He was crushed for our wrongdoings;
The punishment for our well-being was laid upon Him,
And by His wounds we are healed.
All of us, like sheep, have gone astray,
Each of us has turned to his own way;

178

But the LORD has caused the wrongdoing of us all
To fall on Him.
He was oppressed and afflicted,
Yet He did not open His mouth;
Like a lamb that is led to slaughter,
And like a sheep that is silent before its shearers,
So He did not open His mouth.
By oppression and judgment He was taken away;
And as for His generation, who considered
That He was cut off from the land of the living
For the wrongdoing of my people, to whom the blow was due?
 And His grave was assigned with wicked men,
Yet He was with a rich man in His death,
Because He had done no violence,
Nor was there any deceit in His mouth.
But the LORD desired
To crush Him, causing Him grief;
If He renders Himself as a guilt offering,
He will see His offspring,
He will prolong His days,
And the good pleasure of the LORD will prosper in His hand.
As a result of the anguish of His soul,
He will see it and be satisfied;
By His knowledge the Righteous One,
My Servant, will justify the many,
For He will bear their wrongdoings." (Isaiah 53: 4 - 11, NASB).

Response of the Thieves

Two thieves were crucified with Jesus at the same place and at the same time The belief of the society was curse to whoever is hung on the cross (tree). Both experienced Jesus as they were next to Him giving them their last opportunity to accept Him as their personal Savior or reject Him as their Lord. They were both exposed to Jesus, however, each of them had differing response. The response of each of them had everlasting consequences on where they spent eternity, either in hell with the devil or in heaven with Christ. One accepted Christ, but the other insulted Him and rejected Him for the last time. Even at His death on the cross Jesus maintained His love for sinners and demonstrated the truth of the saying in Lamentation, "Because of the LORD's great love we are not consumed, for his compassions never fail. They are new every morning; great is your faithfulness" (Lamentation 3: 22 – 23, NASB).

Judas Iscariot's Response to his Betrayal of Jesus

Judas held a trusted position in Jesus' ministry, he was the treasurer. As a treasurer Judas must have possessed the following qualities, be capable of handling figures and cash; have an orderly mind and methodical way of thinking; have experience of financial control and budgeting; show good time-keeping; have an eye for detail; be available to be contacted for ad hoc advice; have experience in dealing with large sums of money and budgets; have a financial qualification or relevant experience; good communication and interpersonal skills; ability to ensure decisions are taken and followed-up. Judas was so good at anything pertaining to money that he valued money and what money could make possible to do than he valued human life or doing good to others. His extreme love of money led him to betray Jesus for thirty pieces of sliver.

At the time of Jesus, 30 pieces of silver was worth a lot for its purchasing power at the time even though it might seem as a small amount of money in today's economy. Judas' greediness for money did not start with the betrayal of Jesus, but prior, before the climax of his betrayal of Jesus. When Jesus was reclining in the house of Simon a woman poured an expensive perfume on Him. "Mary then took a pound of very expensive perfume of pure nard and anointed the feet of Jesus and wiped His feet with her hair; and the house was filled with the fragrance of the perfume. But Judas Iscariot, one of His disciples, the one who intended to betray Him, said, Why was this perfume not sold for three hundred denarii and the proceeds be given to poor people? Now he said this, not because he cared about the poor, but because he was a thief, and as he kept the money box, he used to steal from what was put into it. Therefore, Jesus said, leave her alone, so that she may keep it for the day of My burial. For you always have the poor with you, but you do not always have Me" (Matthew 26: 6 – 13; Mark 14: 3 - 9, NASB; NIV). Judas Iscariot displayed his love for money in his indignation with the woman's service to Christ. He considered it to be a waste of money which could have been used to take care of the poor as if he cared for the poor. His pretense of caring for the poor was a ploy to have more funds at his disposer to dip into. However, his motive was not pure since he was the treasurer with access to all the funds of the group.

"Then one of the twelve, named Judas Iscariot, went to the chief priests and said, What are you willing to give me to betray Him to you?" And they set out for him thirty pieces of silver. And from then on, he looked for a good opportunity to betray Jesus" (Matthew 26: 14 – 16, NIV). It was his love and greediness for money which led him to betray Jesus. What could have happened to Judas Iscariot if he had repented of his sin of betrayal of Jesus and had he truly asked for forgiveness! From the known qualities of God, there was not a sin that He could not forgive. "If we confess our sins, He is faithful and righteous, so that He will forgive us our sins and cleanse us from all unrighteousness" (John 1: 9, NASB). Even though Judas Iscariot betrayed Jesus He would have been forgiven and Jesus would have carried his sin with the sins of the world as he died on the cross. However, he neither confessed nor asked for the forgiveness of his sin. But, instead of him to run to God in seeking forgiveness he went back to the world, to his collaborators who could not save him and who rejected him. Judas Iscariot still had opportunity to be saved from his sin, but he ignored the opportunity available to him, disappointed by his collaborators and as a result he killed himself without taking advantage of the forgiveness available in store for him. Judas missed the mark of salvation and he perished. God knows how unreliable humans were/are, therefore, he warned all in their reliance on human beings in the following scriptures: "Do not trust a neighbor; put no confidence in a friend. Even with the woman who lies in your embrace, guard the words of your lips" (Micah 7: 5, NIV); "Do not put your trust in princes, in human beings, who cannot save. When their spirit departs, they return to the ground; on that very day their plans come to nothing. Blessed are those whose help is the God of Jacob, whose hope is in the LORD their God" (Psalm 146: 3 – 5, NIV). It is better to trust in the LORD than to put confidence in man. It is better to trust in the LORD than to put confidence in princes" (Psalm 118: 8 – 9, KJV); "This is what the LORD says: "Cursed is the one who trusts in man, who depends on flesh for his strength and whose heart turns away from the LORD. He will be like a bush in the wastelands; he will not see prosperity when it comes. But blessed is the man who trusts in the LORD, whose confidence is in him" (Jeremiah 17: 5, NIV).

"My hope is built on nothing less
Than Jesus' blood and righteousness.
I dare not trust the sweetest frame,
But wholly lean on Jesus' Name.
On Christ the solid Rock I stand,
All other ground is sinking sand;
All other ground is sinking sand.
When darkness seems to hide His face,
I rest on His unchanging grace.
In every high and stormy gale,
My anchor holds within the veil.
On Christ the solid Rock I stand,
All other ground is sinking sand;
All other ground is sinking sand.
His oath, His covenant, His blood,
Support me in the whelming flood.
When all around my soul gives way,
He then is all my hope and stay.
On Christ the solid Rock I stand,
All other ground is sinking sand;

All other ground is sinking sand.
When He shall come with trumpet sound,
Oh may I then in Him be found.
Dressed in His righteousness alone,
Faultless to stand before the throne.
On Christ the solid Rock I stand,
All other ground is sinking sand;
All other ground is sinking sand" (Edward Mote, 1834).

Admonition by the words of God made plain that God is the only One who is always reliable and the support of Whom all humans could truthfully rely on for unwavering support. As stated by Edward Mote in the hymn above trusting in Christ is equivalent to standing on the solid rock, but to do otherwise is standing on the sand which is sinking and is unable to hold anyone up. Judas decided to stand on the sinking sand and that response led to his eternal demise. On which ground are you standing and on who is your hope built?

Responses of Ananias and Sapphira

All the believers were living in one accord. And sharing with each other. Whatever any members of the believers had become a common property of all. Abundant grace was falling on all of them through the preaching and testimony to the resurrection and the power of Jesus Christ. Those in the congregation of believers, if they had land or houses sold them and brought the proceed to the apostles to distribute to the needy ones among them. The generosity of the rich ones among them made it possible for the poor ones among them to live comfortably. (Acts of the Apostles 4: 32 - 35). A couple in the congregation was impressed with what they could see with their eyes and the examples shown by all the rich ones among them who were readily giving of their wealth to the betterment of the believers. The couple, Ananias and Sapphira, wanted to share in the glory and possibly the recognition accorded those who had freely given of their resources to the group. Their response was fraudulent. Although they wanted to share in the glory of giving, they were not fully committed to give all to the group as other givers had done, but only a portion of the proceed of their sale and they lied about the percentage of their giving. All they wanted was the praise of the people. They were doing it as a showoff to the congregation. Therefore, Ananias and Sapphira decided to sell a piece of property, but instead of bringing the entire proceeds as prior donors did they kept back a portion. They conspired together to deceive the congregation and to still get the glory of giving as others who had given wholeheartedly. They wanted to get the praise fraudulently. The Holy Spirit must have hinted the apostles of the fraudulent plot of the couple. The husband must have gone proudly, straight through the congregation and arrogantly to the apostles and laid down his family's present before the apostles to share with the congregation of believers. Peter rebuked him of his hypocrisy, and he died instantaneously. The wife not being aware of what had happened to her husband because of his deceitful response to the apostles came in. When Peter inquired of her, how much the proceed from the sale of their property was, she maintained, in her response to Peter, similar falsehood which led to the death of her husband. As a result of her falsehood response to Peter, he rebuked her, and she met similar fate as her husband due to her untruthful response to Peter's enquiry. (Acts of the Apostles 5: 1 - 11, NASB). Jesus warned His hearers of being hypocritical and of giving gifts or doing good deeds for the praise of people when He said the following: "Take care not to practice your righteousness in the sight of people, to be noticed by them; otherwise, you have no reward with your Father who is in heaven. So, when you give to the poor, do not sound a trumpet before you, as the hypocrites do in the synagogues and on the streets, so that people will praise them. Truly I say to you, they have their reward in full. But when you give to the poor, do not let your left hand know what your right hand is doing, so that your charitable giving will be in secret; and your Father who sees what is done in secret will reward you" (Matthew 6: 1 - 4, NASB). Ananias and Sapphira did not get the praise of the people which was what they desired and even if there was any praise coming their way, they were not alive to enjoy it. They forfeited their lives for nothing just as Jesus said in this teaching, " For what good will it do a person if he gains the whole world, but forfeits his soul? Or what will a person give in exchange for his soul? (Matthew 16: 26 - NASB). "For what does it benefit a person to gain the whole world, and forfeit his soul? (Mark 8: 36, NASB). Ananias and Sapphire denied themselves the opportunity to be of service to God through giving of their resources and they denied others of the benefits others might have received from their stewardship and generosity. The overall consequences of their responses were the losses of their lives and the proceeds they held back from their sale could not save them and it was of no use to them, after all.

Response to Conflict Between Believers

There was a conflict between two groups of the early believers of God. The conflict was getting in the way of doing the work of God and preaching the gospel to the unbelievers. The conflict could have easily put the believers against each other and caused disunity and a show of animosity between them. The conflict could have caused lack of unity of purpose. The disunity could have been so visible to the unbelievers to the detriment of getting non-believers to join their rank. This conflict arose because of the increase in the number of believers which made one group feel that the assistance being given was not extended adequately to their group. In a situation of this nature, it is paramount that the leaders listen to each group and respond with a fair and quick decision to satisfy all sides. The complaint arose by the Hellenistic Jews against the native Hebrews. In the complaint, the Hellenistic Jews felt that their widows were being neglected in the daily food ration. Whenever there is a conflict in the congregation it is important for the leaders to act quickly, as was done in this occasion, so that the problem does fester and become bigger. The leaders of this group called a meeting of everyone to fully understand the problem by hearing from those concerned and to find a way to resolve the issue amicably. The leaders realized that if they fail to resolve the issue promptly it could prevent them from doing the work of God which was their primary mission and not arguing over petty issues. The agreement at the meeting was to select from among the congregation seven men of good reputation, full of the Spirit, and of wisdom to put in charge of the daily food rationing. The congregation was incredibly pleased with the resolution, and they chose seven men among them who met the pre-qualifications as agreed to in the meeting. They prayed and laid hands on the men selected as a commission to perform the responsibility to which they had been selected (Acts of the Apostles 6: 1 - 7, NASB). The quick response of the leaders quenched the festering problem which could have occupied their time and thus preventing them from performing the work of God. The quick action of the leaders improved the unity of the group. The quick response of the leaders to the issue served as a notable example to the outsiders to whom they were preaching. This serves as a splendid example of how Church leaders should respond and resolve issues. "The word of God kept spreading; and the number of the disciples continued to increase greatly in Jerusalem, and a great many of the priests were becoming obedient to the faith" (The Acts of the Apostles 6: 1 - 6, NASB).

Response of Stephen at His Stoning

Stephen was one of the seven men selected by the congregation to be responsible for food rationings to the Hellenistic Hebrew and the native Jewish widows. Stephen had good reputation, he was full of the Spirit, and he possessed great wisdom. "Stephen was full of grace and power, and he was performing great wonders among the people" An opposition arose against him from some men from the Synagogue of the Freedmen from Cyrenius and Alexandrians, from Cicilia and Asia. They went to Stephen because they were jealous of his popularity. They went to him to prove that he was inferior to them, therefore, they argued with him to diminish his status with the people. However, they quickly discovered that Stephen was smarter than them and that they could not match the Spirit by which he was speaking. Therefore, they employed false witnesses to declare that they heard Stephen blasphemous words against Moses and God, knowing that such declaration would make people rise against Stephen. Their consideration worked in the fact that the people, the elders, and the scribes arrested Stephen, presented him to the council, and repeated the same false accusation. They falsely accused him of preaching about Jesus the Nazarene that Jesus of Nazarene would destroy their place and change the law which Moses gave them. Upon hearing those false accusations, the people present were furiously upset at Stephen. "But he, being full of the Holy Spirit, looked intently into heaven and saw the glory of God, and Jesus standing at the right hand of God." In Stephen's response he told them all that happened from Abraham to Moses, and he concluded his defense by saying "You stubborn and hardheaded people! You are always fighting against the Holy Spirit, just as your ancestors did. Is there one prophet that your ancestors didn't mistreat? They killed the prophets who told about the coming of the One Who Obeys God. And now you have turned against him and killed him. Angels gave you God's Law, but you still don't obey it" (Acts of the

Apostles 7: 1-53, NASB) When they heard Stephen's words, they were infuriated, and they attacked him. They dragged him out of the city, and they started throwing stones at him. "As Stephen was being stoned to death, he called out, Lord Jesus, please welcome me! He knelt down and shouted, Lord, don't blame them for what they have done. Then he died" (Acts of the Apostles 7: 54 - 59, NASB).

Paul and Silas Responses to their Imprisonment

Paul and Silas went on their way to a place of prayer to pray, a slave woman who had a spirit of divination which was bringing great profit to her masters by fortune-telling met them and continued to follow them. She was being influenced by the evil spirit dwelling in her and she became a nuisance to them. However, Paul and Silas responded with compassion and in the name of Jesus Christ cast the evil spirit out of her. The owner of the slave woman was not happy because his source of income was depleted by their healing, therefore, he turned Paul and Silas over to the officials. They falsely accused them of bringing Jewish teachings to the Romans. The officials stripped Paul and Silas of their clothes and struck them with many blows in the marketplace before throwing them into prison. The officials instructed the jailers to be sure that they kept Paul and Silas secure in prison to prevent them from escaping. In complying with the command of the officials, the jailer threw Paul and Silas into the inner prison and fastened their feet in the stocks. (Acts of the Apostles 16: 16 - 24, NASB)).

After being beating with clothes off, their skin must have been broken and their bodies must have been full of festering wounds. There was no evidence that their wounds were treated, and such treatment exposed them to infections. they had broken skins and wounds which were untreated, and they must have been uncomfortable and presumably in a lot of pain and discomfort. However, they did not allow their physical and emotional conditions to prevent them from reaching out to God in their pain and distress. They responded while in bondage and in chains in the prison by reaching out to God in prayers and in praising God by singing hymns in devotion of praise. Even in their bondage they were entertaining the prisoners who were listening to them. Their responses to their imprisonment might have appeared strange to other prisoners who were listening to them, and it might have made a great impression on them and eventually leading them to believe in God. God did not forget their plight in prison, and He did not relent in rescuing them because of their response in devotion to Him. God could have quietly rescued them from the prison without a spectacular showing of His power, but He wanted the officials, the jailers, and the prisoners to know that His mighty power could not be deterred by the power and schemes of humans. Therefore, God sent a great earthquake which shook the foundations of the prison, opened all the doors of the prison, and unfastened the chains holding the prisoners down.

They were free through the Almighty power of God brought about by the responses of Paul and Silas in their devotion to God (Acts of the Apostles 16: 25 - 26, NASB).

Upon waking up from his trance and seeing that all the doors of the prison opened, the jailer perceived that all the prisoners had escaped, therefore, he thought that it was better for him to die than to live. The jailer then proceeded to kill himself with his own sword, but Paul and Silas stopped him from harming himself. Paul's and Silas' responses were not of retaliation but of saving the jailer. The jailer was sure that he would face severe punishment up to torture and death by the officials for allowing the prisoners to escape, especially Paul and Silas. "But Paul called out with a loud voice, saying, do not harm yourself, for we are all here! And the jailer asked for lights and rushed in, and trembling with fear, he fell down before Paul and Silas and after he brought them out, he said, Sirs, what must I do to be saved?" (Acts of the Apostles 16: 27 - 30, NASB).

The jailer who had not believed in God up to that point noticed that something was extremely different in the lives of Paul and Silas, he must be thinking that if he were them, he would have run away at the first opportunity available to escape, but to his surprise they did not flee. He must have been impressed by the way they managed their imprisonment through singing and praising God. However, the climax came when they had opportunities to escape, but instead of escaping, they responded with calmness and stayed. The jailer realized that they had something in them which he lacked, he realized that they were saved, and he wanted to know what he needed to do to be saved just as they were. They let him know that what he lacked was the belief in the Lord Jesus Christ. Therefore, they admonished him to believe in the Lord Jesus Christ and that not only him would be saved but his entire household would be saved. Upon hearing the inclusion of his family in the salvation plan he performed the act of kindness on them he then took them straight to his house to meet his family. Paul and Silas preached the word of God to him, and his household, and they all believed and were baptized (Act of the Apostles 16: 31 - 34, NASB). They were all filled with the joy of the Lord. Paul and Silas did not allow anything to separate them from the love of God and while they were in prison, they allowed their light to shine before the jailer and other prisoners while giving glory to the God of Heaven. Paul later wrote: " Who will separate us from the love of Christ? Will tribulation, or trouble, or persecution, or famine, or nakedness, or danger, or sword?" (Romans 8:35, NASB). Their exemplary Christian responses while in prison yielded a great harvest in the kingdom of God. They were not being referent to God to please people or for showoff to others who were watching them, but to show their devotion to God, their deliverer.

The responses of Paul and Silas to their situations were in line with the lyrics of a hymn which says:

1. *While passing through this world of sin,*
And others your life shall view;
Be clean and pure without, within,
Let others see Jesus in you.

Chorus:

Let others see Jesus in you,
Let others see Jesus in you;
Keep telling the story, be faithful and true.
Let others see Jesus in you.

2. *Your life is a book before their eyes,*
They're reading it through and through;
Say, does it point them to the skies,
Do others see Jesus in you?

Chorus:

Let others see Jesus in you ...

3. *What joy 'twill be at set of sun,*
In mansions beyond the blue,
To find some souls that you have won;
Let others see Jesus in you.

Chorus:

Let others see Jesus in you ...

4. *Then live for Christ both day and night,*
Be faithful, be brave, and true,
And lead the lost to life and light;
Let others see Jesus in you.

Chorus:

Let others see Jesus in you ...

Baptist Hymnal 2008 #363.

Response to Thorn in the Flesh

The Bible did not specify what the thorn in the flesh which Paul prayed for was. As a result of lack of clarification by Paul, the problem Paul was facing was left to speculations. However, the clarity of the problem was not as important as Paul's response to his problem. Individual has one problem or the other and an individual handles such problems in many ways. There are healthy ways of dealing with issues and there are unhealthy ways of dealing with issues. The way non-Christians deal with issues is completely different from the ways Christians deal or should deal with problems. Non-Christian deal with problems for most times in unhealthy ways. Since non-Christians do not have their foundation on faith on the Holy God, they relied on the ways of the world to deal with their problems. Instead of crying to God they rely on other unhealthy means to mask their problems. They might rely on drugs, alcohol, and other earthly means which neither resolve their problems nor give them any lasting satisfaction and solution once the masking is removed. Christians on the other hand rely or should rely on partnership with God to resolve their problems. Christians should turn to God, to their Bibles, and to other Christians to join them in prayers to resolve their problems. Instead of employing the ways of the world Christians should respond to problems by getting God involved in what they are neither able nor have resources enough to handle. This was the example and the legacy left by Paul with his resolution of the thorn in the flesh. Paul declared that he prayed for the problem to be removed but the problem persisted. However, Paul was not discouraged, but he moved closer to God. Paul did not abandon God, but he relied on God for strength to endure his problem. Even though Paul considered himself weak, but he relied on the power and strength of God. Paul's action should be a model for how Christians should handle problems, although that response might not be easy, Christians cannot do it on their own power,

196

but through the power of God who gives strength. Paul not only demonstrated his reliance on God by his actions but also in his words when he stated in Philippians 4:13, (GWT) thus, "I can do everything through Christ who strengthens me."

"Because of the surpassing greatness of the revelations, for this reason, to keep me from exalting myself, there was given me a thorn in the flesh, a messenger of Satan to torment me to keep me from exalting myself! Concerning this I implored the Lord three times that it might leave me. And He has said to me, My grace is sufficient for you, for power is perfected in weakness. Most gladly, therefore, I will rather boast about my weaknesses, so that the power of Christ may dwell in me. Therefore, I am well content with weaknesses, with insults, with distresses, with persecutions, with difficulties, for Christ's sake; for when I am weak, then I am strong" (2 Corinthians 12: 7 - 10, NASB). Paul considered his problem as a way to keep him humble before God and before others. Paul's response to his problem was the development of humility and a reliance on God.

Response to Nagging Emotional Irritants

There are several forms of what appears to be constant nagging emotional irritants in all forms of relationships. Although there will always be some form of emotional irritants in human relationships, how individual responds to those persistent nagging irritants could make a significant difference in the outcomes. There is a saying that if life presents you with a lemon, you should make lemonade out of it. 'Lemon,' in this case is a metaphor for an unpleasant issue. It is a messy situation out of which one should respond by turning the mess into a message - a message full of grace. There appears to be regular irritants with those in close relationship such as family members, the spouse, the children, and friends, and other close individuals. A popular pastor once made a statement in his preaching about an argument between him and his spouse. The argument was so pronounced that the spouse locked herself in the bathroom. They could hear each other with the pastor outside the door of the bathroom. As they were yelling at each other, according to the pastor, he said that he remarked to his wife – "everyone thinks that I am the greatest, but it is only you who think differently." The wife responded to him by saying, "it is because they do not either live with you or know you as much as I know you." This response gave the pastor an introspection of himself and realized that he needed to make a change. He needed to treat his wife as well as he treats the outsiders. The pastor apologized for his behavior and realized that the kindness he has been extending to the outsiders should be extended to those in his household, with his spouse and with his children. This is a common theme to human relationship. People are more understanding and more tolerant in their responses and their behavior to those outside their household than to those who are in their household. This should not be so. It is in the home that spouses second guess the motives of each other. it is where parents and children are not forgiving of each other. This should not

198

be so. Whenever one member of a relationship assigns motives to the action of another member the response hardly ends positively. James had valuable pieces of advice, first to Christians which could be extended to non-Christians by the way Christians respond to issues between them and non-Christians - your response could make a difference on whether they believe and accept God or not, therefore, watch how you respond.

Watch how you respond to others, are your responses encouraging or discouraging., are they edifying or not? A story was told of a father whose very young son was very excited to tell him of his first-time toy putting together achievements. The son had worked hard to complete putting together a toy he got as a gift. He was very eager to show his expertise to his dad upon his return from work. He could hardly wait for his father to come home and appreciate his handwork. Upon hearing the motor of his father's car stopped on the driveway of their home. He opened the blind of the window of his room to see the driveway of their home. Upon realizing that his father just arrived at home he opened the door faster for his father than he has ever done in the past with the anticipation to show his newly put together toy car to his father. The boy ran back into his room, took the toy car off his bed, and returned speedily to present his toy car proudly to his father. Unfortunately, the father 'looked down' on the achievement of his son and instead of being excited with him he belittled the accomplishments of which the boy was very excitedly proud, and he said, "Is that the best you could do?" The son was so disappointed at his father's response, went back to his room to weep in sadness. The son was so discouraged that he never put another toy together again. The father's response to the hard work of his son had a tremendous lasting negative impact on his interest on being innovative. This type of response might not be limited to parent child relationship, but could be between spouses, family members, friends, and acquaintances. If one person in a relationship has been persuading the other to perform an action for quite a while and the other person finally does it, the response should be of elation and happiness even if the action appears to be a small step towards the major goal. Appreciation and encouragement could go a long way in continuing and in improving the action. However, if the response is in the form of, 'it is about time' or 'you finally got to it' or any form of sarcastic comments, the action might never continue, and the relationship might be injured if not destroyed. Even in animal training, encouragement is used in form of giving appropriate rewards or withdrawal of reward to stiffen an action. What is your response to what appears small steps of achievement, are you an encourager or a discourager? In majority of Paul's writings, he greeted and encouraged the Churches. God expects Christians to be encouragers to all their acquaintances in the home or outside the home. "Do not let any unwholesome talk come out of your mouths, but only what is helpful for building others up according to their needs, that it may benefit those who listen. Not that I have attained it but pursuing it" (Philippians 3: 13-14, NASB). It is important to allow Christ to direct the words coming out of one's mouth and for those words to be edifying and to lift others up. In Paul's admonition he said, " Be wise in the way you act toward outsiders; make the most of every opportunity. Let your conversation be full of grace, seasoned with salt, so that you may know how to answer everyone' (Colossians 4: 5 - 6, NASB).

"Some days life feels perfect
Other days, it just ain't workin'
The good, the bad, the right, the wrong
And everything in between
Though it's crazy, amazing
We can turn our hearts through the words we say
Mountains crumble with every syllable
Hope can live or die
So, speak life, speak life
To the deadest darkest night
Speak life, Speak life
When the sun won't shine and you don't know why
Look into the eyes of the brokenhearted
Watch 'em come alive as soon as you speak hope
You speak love, you speak
You speak life, oh, oh, oh, oh, oh
You speak life, oh, oh, oh, oh, oh
Some days, the tongue got twisted

Other days, my thoughts just fall apart
I do, I don't, I will, I won't
It's like I'm drowning in the deep
Well, it's crazy to imagine
Words from my lips as the arms of compassion
Mountains crumble with every syllable
Hope can live or die
So, speak life, speak life
To the deadest darkest night
Speak life, Speak life
When the sun won't shine, and you don't know why
Look unto the eyes of the broken hearted
Watch 'em come alive as soon as you speak hope
You speak love, you speak, oh, oh, oh, oh, oh
You speak life, oh, oh, oh, oh, oh
Lift your head a little higher
Spread the love like fire
Hope will fall like rain
When you speak life with the words you say
Raise your thoughts a little higher
Use your words to inspire
Joy will fall like rain
When you speak life with the things you say
Lift your head a little higher
Spread the love like fire
Hope will fall like rain
When you speak life with the words you say
So, speak life, speak life
To the deadest darkest night
Speak life, speak life
When the sun won't shine and you don't know why
Look into the eyes of the brokenhearted
Watch 'em come alive as soon as you speak hope
You speak love, you speak
You speak Life, you speak Life
You speak life, oh, oh, oh, oh, oh
You speak Life, oh, oh, oh, oh, oh

You speak Life, oh, oh, oh, oh, oh
You speak Life, oh, oh, oh, oh, oh
Some days life feels perfect" (TobyMac).

The lyric of the song above should remind all to speak life not only when everything is going well, but when things are going bad, not when other people are kind, but also when they are unkind, not only when the going is good, but also when the going is bad and one could not fathom why it was so. The responses in good words coming out of one's mouth should not be limited to the good times only, but also in troubled times, not only at the time of success, but at the time of failure, as well. The words coming out one's mouth should give hope, life, inspiration, encouragement, stimulation, empowerment, and love to the downhearted. It is important that the words coming from a person's mouth be edifying to the hearers. In Titus 2: 7 - 8 (NASB) Paul instructed Titus to be an example of honorable deeds, showing integrity in teaching, seriousness and soundness in speech which are above condemnation thus putting to shame the opposition

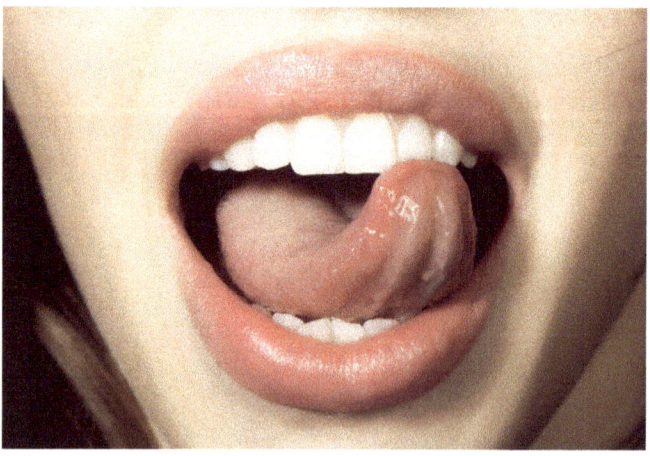

when they found nothing bad about Christians.

James warned of the evils of the careless use of the tongue. He compared the tongue to a small fire which could destroy a big forest. The tongue is exceedingly small compared to many other parts of the body, but it could cause a very great havoc to the rest of the body. The tongue could start wars and it could end wars. The tongue could bring about destruction to the whole body. The tongue if not subjected to the control of God could go wild and remain untamed. Sea animals, land animals, and birds of the air could be tamed but the tongue could go wild unless it is put under God's subjection to be tamed. The tongue left uncontrolled by God could be full of deadly poison used to curse people. However, when the tongue is subjected to God's control it could be used to praise God and bless people. Responses emanating from a God controlled tongue is edifying to the hearers and seasoned with salt. God expects humans to use their tongues only for good words and not for evil (James 3: 5 - 12, NASB); (Ephesians 4: 29, NIV).There are several persistent nagging emotional irritants in the home which require the direction from God to appreciate the value of the relationships, and to have humility to navigate the irritants daily. Human relationships are froth with irritants which need constant adjusting and re-adjusting through the wisdom which comes only from God. "But if any of you lacks wisdom, let him ask of God, who gives to all generously and without reproach, and it will be given to him" (James 1: 5, NASB). An example of a persistent nagging emotional irritant in the home could be such things as how the toothpaste is squeezed out of the tube. James had valuable pieces of advice, first to Christians which could be extended to non-Christians by the way Christians respond to issues between them and non-Christians - your response could make a difference on whether they believe and accept God or not, therefore, watch how you respond. A spouse might be diligent in squeezing the tooth paste from the bottom/base to get the tooth paste by pushing it forward methodically. However, the other spouse might always squeeze the toothpaste tube from the middle and seemingly

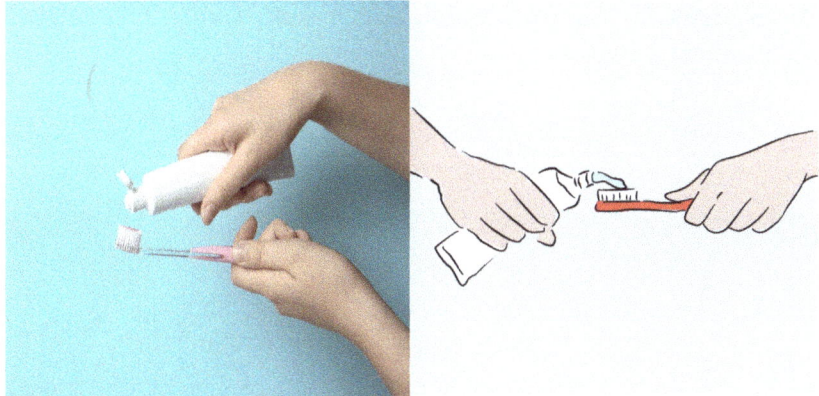

undoing the methodical use of squeezing the tooth paste out. This could be irritable to the other spouse. This insignificant issue could be the start of a significant problem for the couple if the response of either was not measured. A similar irritant could be the way the toilet paper is put on the toilet paper dispenser.

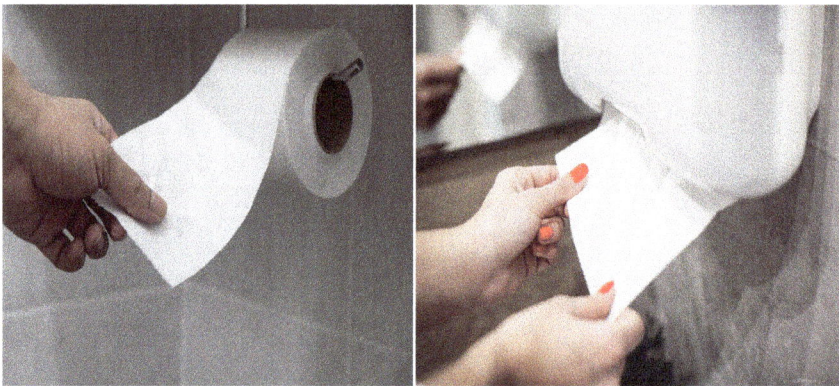

A spouse might always put the toilet paper to come from over the toilet paper dispenser whereas the other spouse might prefer to have the toilet paper come from under the toilet paper dispenser. It might occur that neither of them speaks out about his or her preference, but each is equally irritated by the practice of the other. One of the spouses might be in the habit of reversing what the other spouse does and to come the next time and see that his or her last action has been reversed by the other spouse. However, without talking about it the irritant between them regarding this issue could continue. It could be 'the candle which ignites' the process of a major problem between them, as little as the issue appears to be. The best solution to any issue is to have a cordial discussion and to respond with understanding and love.

Children in the Family

"Behold, children are a gift of the LORD,
The fruit of the womb is a reward.
 Like arrows in the hand of a warrior,
So are the children of one's youth.
Blessed is the man whose quiver is full of them;
They will not be ashamed
When they speak with their enemies in the gate
Behold, children are a gift of the LORD,
The fruit of the womb is a reward.
Like arrows in the hand of a warrior,
So are the children of one's youth.
Blessed is the man whose quiver is full of them;
They will not be ashamed
Chilldren are the gift from the Lord

When they speak with their enemies in the gate. Lord " (Psalm 127: 3 - 5, NASB). Children are blessings from God, however, with every blessing God expects responsibilities. God puts parent(s) in charge of their children, and He expects them to raise them in reference to Him. Parents are to teach their child/children about God, their relationships to their neighbor and those who they have abilities to assist. In dealing with neighbors, people should go by Jesus description of a neighbor in the parable of the Good Samaritan. Parents are to show good examples in words and deeds. Parents will be held responsible for how they raise their children and in that case, what is a blessing could become a curse. Parents should maintain a good relationship worthy of emulation by the child or children. Behaviors of the father and the mother should be such that are good for the little eyes to see during the times when things are going well and during the times when things are not going so well. The father and mother should have plans and processes to follow in raising their children in accordance with the will of God. One parent should not override the other in dealing with issues and outcomes pertaining to their child or children. If one parent says no to the child's or children's want(s) in the absence of the other parent, the child or children is or are good at going to the other parent who was not present and seek permission for the same issue(s), hoping that the other parent would respond positively to the request(s). The response of the parent who was not present should be, have you asked mom or dad before giving the positive response to what is/ are being requested. If the response from the child or children is yes, the next question should be what did mom or dad say? This will force the child or children to disclose what mom or dad said. The last parent should not give a response other than to tell the child or children that he or she would talk with the first parent and come up with a response for the child or children. The parents should then have a conference in the absence of the child or children and come up with a unified response which both will give to the child or children jointly at the same time. This unified response would prevent the child or children from playing one parent against the other. At times, misunderstanding could happen between the parents when the child/children are present, in that case, the parents should be measured in their responses to each other. If the issue has the potential to go bad, the parents should postpone further conversation about it until the child or children are not present. This should not be a regular practice when there are issues for discussion in the presence of the child or children on every difficult issue to be resolved. The parents should be able to resolve issues amicably in the presence of the child or children in order to serve as models to the child or children. The child or children would begin to see how mom and dad resolve issues and they would emulate it in their future issue resolutions. The way parents respond to issue could serve as building blocks for the character formation of their child or children. It is important for parents not to show favoritism for one child over another, but to treat every child equally, even though each child's personality could be different from the other. However, parents should treat each child according to each child's personality, a statement that could be accepted by one child might be repugnant to the other. Although they are children of the same parents each child's personality might be different. The parents should know and understand each child to customize handling each child based on the child's personality without favoritism. The personality for a male child might be different from the personality of the female child, therefore, gender might be considered in managing the children. Parents responses to the child or children could make a difference in the personality development of each child, therefore, parents' responses should always be positive when disciplining the child or children is necessary. Discipline should always be done with love. "And have you forgotten the exhortation that addresses you as sons? My son do not regard lightly the discipline of the Lord, nor be weary when reproved by him. For the Lord disciplines the one he loves and chastises every son whom he receives. It is for discipline that you have to endure. God is treating you as sons. For what son is there whom his father does not discipline? If you are left without discipline, in which all have participated, then you are illegitimate children and not sons" (Hebrews 12: 5-8, ESV). God showed humans His love when there was/is need for discipline, therefore, parent should discipline with love as God disciplines them in love. Whenever humans follow the example of God in whatever they do they will always do it right. For God said treat others as you will like to be treated.

Children's personalities are, generally, different one from the other even though they are from the same father and mother within a family, even if there are only two children. Therefore, the more children the parents have the more juggling acts between different personalities of the children the parents must be ready to maneuver. It appears that having two children does not present so much of a challenge for parents of two children, probably because there are only two personalities to master and because it is very possible to give about as much equal attention to each of the two children without any of them being left out or feeling as being left out. A family with three children has a bigger challenge to face so that the middle child does not feel as being cheated out of the attention he/she deserves. A middle child might feel that before he or she was born his older sibling got undivided attention of their parents and when he or she was born, he/she could not get the full attention of the parents because his parents have to share their attention between both of them. The middle child might be getting used to this situation until the third child arrives and demands the attention of their parents. It might come to a point when the youngest sibling needs more attention and receives more attention from their parents than either of the older siblings. The middle child might be caught in the middle. The middle child might feel that there was no time when he/she ever fully got the attention of their parents alone and might feel cheated. The parents must be cognitive of this phenomenon to pay special attention to the middle child. As a result of this feeling the middle child might develop what is called middle-child syndrome which might not reveal itself until sometimes later in the life of the middle child. Each middle child deals with the middle-child syndrome differently. Some middle children might have increased incentive to exceed while others might deal with it with discouragement. It is the responsibility of parents to be mindful of the middle-child syndrome to give equal attention to each of the three children as each needs so that none of the children feels left out of the attention of their parents. Such response from the parents could help in inducing positive character developments of each of the three children without any of them feeling left out. According to Alfred Adler, a psychologist, middle-child-syndrome might be more pronounced in males than in females. He associated the following characteristic traits to middle children: They are sociable and are good mediators as they can see more than one side of an issue and seek fairness for all involved. They are great negotiators. Middle children are outstanding, and they learn how to act and make friends. They learn easily from their siblings and peers and as a result improve themselves. However, middle children might feel overshadowed by their siblings and might feel a stronger sense of not belonging than their siblings. Middle children might move out of the house earlier than their siblings. They might embark on something which their siblings are not good at doing. Due to their inherent feelings of middle children as being deprived of the full attention of their parents it is paramount that parents with middle child/children seek God's guidance in racing middle children and avoid an appearance of showing favoritism to either of the children. May the Lord help.

Response to 'Front Seat' Passenger Driver'

A 'front seat passenger driver' could be a blessing at times, however, in most cases he/she could be a constant irritant or detractor. Everyone needs a space and freedom to operate independently without anyone looking over his/her shoulders. But the 'front seat passenger driver' has the tendency to want to be in control even when someone else is driving. He/she appears to be a perfect driver and as a result wants to constantly coach the driver on what is happening, what to do, and how to do it. What the 'front seat passenger driver' forgets to realize is that he or she does not know the thinking of the driver and that the driver could see the situation around the car better in his or her vantage than the 'front seat passenger driver' could see. Even with that fact being obvious or pointed out, the 'front seat passenger driver' continues to interject his or her opinion into the driving process. It is difficult for the driver to operate the vehicle independently which is what is needed for a safe driving of the vehicle when a 'front seat passenger driver' is present. The unwelcome pieces of advice, interjections, expertise of the 'front seat passenger driver 'makes operating a vehicle annoying and less enjoyable for the driver and it could result in unwanted mishap. The 'front seat passenger driver' who has been accustomed to the overpowering behavior finds it difficult to resist despite the driver's display of dislike for such behavior. In occasions when there will be multiple passengers in the vehicle, the driver would prefer the 'front seat passenger driver' to seat at the back of the vehicle rather than in front with the driver. This strategy might work at times, but it could not be counted on as having chances to always succeed. Since it is difficult to change the habit of the 'front seat passenger driver' how should the driver respond to the nagging irritation which is certain to come from the 'front seat passenger driver'? In frustrating situations James has the following pieces of advice to everyone who is a recipient of such treatment, his piece of advice involves patience. He compared the patience needed by an individual to a "farmer who plants crops but waits patiently for the precious produce of the soil, being patient about it, until it gets the early and late rains. You too be patient; strengthen your hearts, for the coming of the Lord is near. Do not complain, brothers and sisters, against one another, so that you may not be judged; behold, the Judge is standing right at the door. As an example, brothers and sisters, of suffering and patience, take the prophets who spoke in the name of the Lord. We count those blessed who endured. You have heard of the endurance of Job and have seen the outcome of the Lord's dealings, that the Lord is full of compassion and is merciful" (James 5: 7 – 11, NASB). God's expectation of the people, especially, Christians on how to respond or treat those who do annoying things or offensive things are not easy to practice. Such patience which God expects people to display to each other could only be achieved through the submission to the direction of the Holy spirit. Without submission to the Holy Spirit, it is impossible to respond patiently as God expects. Therefore, whenever you are in an irritating situation directed against you, pause, and quickly seek God's direction on how to respond appropriately. This practice might not be satisfying at the beginning, but with frequent practice will become more satisfying.

Effects of Outside Issues on Family Responses

The advent of cell phones has made life easier and communication readily available regardless of distance. Although cell phone is a blessing it could also be a curse and a source of problems in the family. Before the improvement on the communication modalities, public pay telephones were the order of the day. Communication was slower and the ability to communicate through electronic means were a matter of hit and miss. One always had to carry appropriate form of coins to be able to operate a public telephone. People were not very reliant on having prompt communication through the telephone.

However, the improvement from public pay telephone to advanced cell phones with texting, emailing, and other capabilities has reduced the patience of people to tolerate slow communications and has increased faster gratification of quicker communications. When this expectation is not met it could create hardship in relationships. A story was told of a couple who took advantage of the prompt communications between the husband and his wife regardless of how far away from each other, they were always able to communicate timely with each other through their cell phones.

However, one spouse was in the habit of laying his cell phone at the last place he was, especially, in their home, for periods of time without the phone being with him at his current location. As a result, he missed some calls on occasions whenever he was in another part of the premises without his cell phone. On one occasion, the wife had a challenging time at work and wanted to share her experiences of the day with her spouse who did not pick up the phone because his phone was not with him at that moment. It was the customary habit of the husband to call his wife to check on her welfare whenever they have been apart from each other for a while. However, on this day he got too busy with other tasks that he lost track of the time and he forgot to call and check on the welfare of his wife. The wife became angry on her way home and the closer she got to home the angrier she became. Upon arriving at home instead of calmly inquiring of what had happened to the husband she got terribly upset with him. She was so upset that she uttered some unkind words out of her mouth against her husband. The husband was 'dumbfounded' and 'flat footed' as to how to respond to the unusual and unexpected behavior of his wife. They both responded to each other with heated unkind words. The exchanges of unkind words to each other continued until their time of togetherness was ruined for the rest of the day. The other day they recounted to each other what had happened the previous day and they each regretted their responses to each other. Each took responsibilities for his/her responses which put 'gasoline on the simmering fire'. The husband was committed to always have his cell phone with him wherever he is. The wife regretted allowing her challenging issues from work to ruin her time with her husband. The wife decided to always leave issues about work at work by clearing her mind of work issues before getting home and never again to allow such issues to ruin her family fellowship. After losing a day of great relationship because of their initial responses to each other this couple reversed course, they realized the folly of their prior responses, apologized to each other, and renewed their relationships. This couple followed the advice of Paul when he said 'BE ANGRY, AND YET DO NOT SIN; do not let the sun go down on your anger, and do not give the devil an opportunity" (Ephesians 4: 26 - 27, NASB). It is not a sin to be angry, however, being angry should be short lived, otherwise, the devil could take advantage of the anger and lead people to do evil. This is a notable example in human relationship on how to resolve issues without dissolving the relationships. In the same likeness James admonished believers in these words, "You know this, my beloved brothers and sisters. Now everyone must be quick to hear, slow to speak, and slow to anger; for a man's anger does not bring about the righteousness of God" (James 1: 19 - 20, NASB). Christians should be good listeners because many breakups of relationships stem from second guessing the other person's motives instead of listening intently and asking clarifying question to be sure that one is not misunderstanding the intent of the other. It is not a good personality trait to get angry easily, especially, anyone who calls himself or herself by the name of Christ should go to God to rid himself or herself of anger to bring about the righteousness of God. Christians should be the light and salt of the world, but this could only be so by bringing about the righteousness of God before the unbelievers.

At Work, how do you deal with the following: An extremely high percentage of the people are normal. Normality in this case means that a high percentage of people do not have malicious intentions to do wrong. However, any human being could commit and does commit errors at times in his/her lifetime. The most important thing is to have an environment where errors could be disclosed quickly at the opportune time to take remedial steps before damages are done because of the error(s). In the healthcare system, especially, it is essential for trust to exist in the work environment whereby staff feel safe to report error(s) promptly instead of hiding it/them. The safety of patients' health depends on prompt reporting of errors on the rare occasions that they do happen. However, prompt reporting of errors depends on the trust that those in power would not punish the staff who has committed the error. When such environment has been created the safety of the patients and the safety of the staff are enhanced. Since healthcare workers and other professionals with similar responsibilities are humans there are tendencies for occasional error(s) to occur. In a book titled "To Err Is Human" the editors, Linda T. Kohn, Janet M. Corrigan, Molla S. Donaldson, emphasized the importance of not blaming or pointing fingers at those who make honest mistakes. Mistakes or errors do occur in any human endeavor, but a quick declaration of errors as they occur could mitigate the adverse effects of the errors. Almost any error could be reversed if reported promptly to those who could do something about it. However, staff will report errors if they trust that there will not be adverse repercussions to them and their employment. The response of the superior when an error is reported promptly will either promote the truthfulness and promptness in reporting errors or hiding them. If the superior's response was of support and understanding the habit of prompt reporting of errors would be encouraged. However, if the response of the superior was

of punishment the spirit of prompt truthful reporting of errors could be dampened. It takes only one incident for the staff to continue the habit of prompt truthfully reporting of errors or hiding the information regarding the occurrence of error(s). Therefore, the response of the superior to the subordinates could have a reverberating effect on truthful prompt error reporting in any line of work. A story was told of a new manager in an Urgent Care Department. The Urgent Care Department was situated on two floors, first and second floors of a healthcare building. The manager had staff on both floors. The new manager, within a short period of time, noticed that the staff did not trust their prior manager and that the lack of trust of the prior manager had been transferred to him. Therefore, the staff were very suspicious of their new manager based on their prior experiences with their former manager. He noticed that whenever he called them to his office on the first floor, they appeared nervous and anxious as to what would happen. After several instances of receiving similar reactions from the staff the new manager did not like the fact that the staff were extremely nervous around him, especially, whenever he called them to his office. Therefore, he was determined to break (dissuade) them of the habit. In this Urgent Care Department, the receptionists gave service evaluation papers to the patients to complete on the healthcare staff who addressed their issues in any capacity. The patients could return the service evaluation papers when completed to the manager on the same day after their visits or mail them back to urgent Care, however, regardless of how they returned them those evaluation papers would go to the manager, eventually. Of those retuned evaluations some would bear good tidings, but some would indicate areas of improvements needed either for the organization or for the individual staff who attended to the patients. Instead of presenting service evaluations results at the staff meeting the manager decided to call each staff to his office as the service evacuation papers came back for each. He could have waited to present all evaluation results at their regular monthly staff meeting, but he decided that a way to break the staff of their nervous attitude around him was to have each of them experience his responses to each in his office whether the service evaluation was good or bad. He would call whichever staff got a service evaluation report over the phone and he would say "I need to have a talk with you in my office as soon as you are able." The staff would run stumbling on himself or herself to the manager's office on the first floor. Upon arriving at the manager's office, the staff would appear very nervous in anticipation of what the issue was. The manager would have the staff sit and he would tell the staff "I called you because of an information I got from a patient who received your service the other day." The manager would then pretend to be looking on his desk for the written information from the patient. The manager was doing that to get the staff to 'work himself or herself up' emotionally for a few minutes. He would then pick up the service evaluation sheet from his desk and open it slowly. As he opens it he would make some noises like – 'hum' with his body gesture in unison. At this point the staff would be sitting nervously expecting the worst. The manager would then stretch out his hand to shake the staff's hand with the word "excellent job." At this point the staff was already in a daze and could hardly hear the word "Good Job". The manager then emphasized on how good a job the staff did in his/her service to the patient. The staff would marvel and ask, "why did you not tell me immediately that it was good news." The manager then responded and said, "whenever I call any of you, I do not want you to be very anxious and nervous coming to me because I want you to know that I am not God. However, whenever I call you, I want you to know that it could be for good news, to seek your opinion on matters I plan to do or to discuss a service which did not go according to patient's expectation. If it were good news, it would be time to celebrate a job well done, if it were for your opinion, it meant that I am seeking your input, or if it were for a service performed below patient's expectation, it was time to strategize on what to do to correct the service to meet the patient's reasonable expectations the next time." The manager did not have to go through many of such sessions before the staff began to appreciate the management style of the new manager and began to trust him. His responses gave the confidence that he was there as a leader who was looking for their best interest, as well as, the best interest of the patients. Whenever he called them to his office, they were no longer nervous but went to him with confidence. Whenever any staff felt that his or her service was below expectation and had some feelings that the patient might lodge a complaint or submit a service evaluation not meeting the patient's expectation the staff would be the first who reports himself or herself to the manager because he or she trusted that her manager would be fair in his response to him or her. Their job performance improved and the service evaluation ratings for the staff from the patients improved for individual staff and for the department. The response of the new manager turned the work environment around positively for all. The behavior and the management style of this manager was congruent with the teaching of Apostle Paul when Paul said, "Brothers and sisters, even if a person is caught in any wrongdoing, you who are spiritual are to restore such a person in a spirit of gentleness; each one looking to yourself, so that you are not tempted as well. Bear one another's burdens, and thereby fulfill the law of Christ. For if anyone thinks that he is something when he is nothing, he deceives himself. But each one must examine his own work, and then he will have reason for boasting, but to himself alone, and not to another. For each one will bear his own load" (Galatians 6: 1 - 4, NASB). The new manager's responses were of kindness and of no harshness to his staff realizing that as a human being he could display poor service to others or make erroneous decisions, as well.

Regardless of how peaceful a person is there could be a perpetrator who would want to test the one, especially, if the perpetrator knows the person to be a Christian. The perpetrator might be picking a fight with the individual Christian to test the Christian's reaction. It might have even been the devil who has his imprint on the action of the perpetrator who is picking a fight with the Christian. However, at that point the Christian needs to look up to God for the appropriate response to the perpetrator. It is important to act instead of reacting because action is deliberate, but reaction is debilitating; action is thoughtful while reaction is impulsive. Action led by God is godly, but reaction is devilish. When one involves God in one's action the result is always positive and rewarding, but reaction does not produce lasting reward and it is not of God. "At that time Jesus went through the grainfields on the Sabbath, and His disciples became hungry and began to pick the heads of grain and eat. Now when the Pharisees saw this, they said to Him, Look, Your disciples are doing what is not lawful to do on a Sabbath! But He said to them, Have you not read what David did when he became hungry, he and his companions how he entered the house of God and they ate the consecrated bread which was not lawful for him to eat nor for those with him, but for the priests alone? Or have you not read in the Law that on the Sabbath the priests in the temple violate the Sabbath, and yet are innocent? But I say to you that something greater than the temple is here. But if you had known what this means: 'I DESIRE COMPASSION, RATHER THAN SACRIFICE,' you would not have condemned the innocent. For the Son of Man is Lord of the Sabbath" (Matthew 12: 1 – 8, NASB). The Pharisees were notorious for picking a fight with Jesus. They kept watching Him not to learn, but to find fault in Him with whatever He or His disciples did. On this occasion on the Sabbath day, they felt that they got Him ready handed through the actions of His disciples, therefore, in an attempt to pick a fight with Jesus, they accused Him about the action of His disciples. However, Jesus did not react to them in the manner they expected, but He acted in a manner controlled by God and appealed to their senses. He reminded them of what they did not know or what they have conveniently forgot or ignored about the action of David. The Pharisees revered David as their king and ancestor, therefore, Jesus pointed to the action of David and those who were with him when they were hungry, went into the temple, and ate the consecrated bread which was not lawful for any of them to eat. Jesus must have mentioned the actions of David and of the priests because those were the ones the Pharisees revered. Instead of Jesus reacting to their accusation he made them to start thinking and that provided Jesus the opportunity to tell them what they lacked, which was compassion. Jesus was telling them that having compassion was better than all their outward superficial actions of sacrifice and worship. There is a great piece of advice in Hebrews for Christians on how to behave when someone is picking on them. God did not put responsibility on the perpetrator, but on the one being picked on. God expects Christians to be good examples to others even when being wronged. This expectation was made clear in these verses, "Pursue peace with all people, and the holiness without which no one will see the Lord. See to it that no one comes short of the grace of God; that no root of bitterness springing up causes trouble, and by it many become defiled" (Hebrews 12: 14 – 15, NASB). Although Jesus was as harmless as a dove, He was very wise. Jesus wanted his followers to imitate Him in all that they did/do, therefore, while sending His disciples on their missionary journey He instructed them "Behold, I send you forth as sheep in the midst of wolves: be ye therefore wise as serpents, and harmless as doves" (Matthew 10: 26, KJV). In the world to which they were going to be exposed Jesus instructed them to be wise just as the serpent, which was the wisest of all animals, however, with that wisdom Jesus expected them to add peace and harmlessness to their character. Jesus wanted them to be the salt of the world to attract the unbelievers to God. Although the unbelievers might be doing wrong to Christians it is the Christian responsibility to pay them with good and to be wise and vigilant.

Response to Those in Power over You

Paul's pieces of advice to believers are to be subject to those in authority. In order words he was telling every believer to listen and obey the Godly directives coming from those in position of authority. Paul expanded on his pieces of advice by saying that anyone in power is put there with the knowledge and permission of God and their authority emanated from God. Paul did not stop with his pieces of advice, but he declared that anyone who resists/opposes authority opposes what God has ordained. The consequence for resisting authority are condemnation on the resistant person. Whoever resists authority should be afraid of the one in authority for the punishment that is forth coming. However, in order not to be afraid of authority everyone should do good and obey authority. "Every person is to be subject to the governing authorities. For there is no authority except from God, and those which exist are established by God. Therefore, whoever resists authority has opposed the ordinance of God; and they who have opposed will receive condemnation upon themselves." (Romans 13: 1 – 2, NASB). Consequences are there for those who refuse to obey authority and refuse to do good. Doing good, Paul said is not only to avoid punishment, but because it is the right thing to do and to have a clear conscience. Paul dived into the issue of taxes and urged believers to pay their due taxes for rulers are servants of God, devoting themselves to this very thing. Paul continued his advice by saying that believers should pay all taxes, customs, respect, and honor to whom those things are due. Believers are not to be in debt to anyone except the debt of love to one another and to their neighbors (a neighbor based on Jesus' definition of a neighbor in the story of the Good Samaritan) is the fulfilment of the law. Paul concluded his pieces of advice by saying that love is the fulfilment of the law. Then Paul summed up the law in this statement by saying, "YOU SHALL LOVE YOUR NEIGHBOR AS YOURSELF. Love does no wrong to a neighbor; therefore love is the fulfillment of the Law" Romans 13: 1 - 10, NASB). Therefore, based on Paul's admonition and reasoning, it is expedient to obey those in authority which includes bosses of employees. The employees should follow the directives from those leaders in order to get high praise, recognition, and good standing on the job. Paul continued his pieces of advice by saying "Whatever you do, do your work heartily, as for the Lord and not for people, knowing that it is from the Lord that you will receive the reward of the inheritance. It is the Lord Christ whom you serve" (Colossians 3; 23 - 24, NASB). Paul's instruction here puts into account that some employees are only diligent in performing their job when there is the boss around, however, they look for opportunities not to work up to their level or as required by the company when there is no one around to monitor them. Paul is saying here that you do not need to have your boss or supervisor around to work as expected of you if you consider that the Lord is your boss. Even if the earthly boss does not see what you do and how well you do it, the Lord sees it all. Since the Lord Jesus Christ who you serve could see the caliber of your performance you should work as if Jesus is your employer. When your response to your job is diligence, the Lord Jesus Christ, as your boss, will reward you abundantly. How do you respond when it appears that you are the only one who attends to the supplies or the items used by all? For example, it might appear that no one else among your coworkers fills up the papers in the copier machine or in the printer paper tray. You have this feeling because it never fails that whenever you want to make copies of documents or print documents, in most cases, the copier machine or the printer is empty of papers. It appears as if you are the only one who cares for the next person, but no one else does. How do you respond to this recurring issue? The issue might not be related to office supplies, but it might be other type of issues to which you feel as if you are the only one who takes responsibility to take care of it, but others benefit from your efforts without lifting a finger to assist, but they are fast to reap the benefits. How do you feel about others who are not helping, but reaping the benefits? How will you let others see Jesus in your response to this type of issues and still get your points across? Do not allow your feelings or emotion to control your response or give God the opportunity to speak through you and He will direct your action and response to make the situation result in a positive outcome.

Gossiping

Gossiping is unauthorized habitual revealing of personal or sensational information of others. The information could be false or factual, but the disclosure or dissemination of the information is not permitted (Merriam-Webster). A gossiper talks about the private affairs of others without first seeking permission. A gossiper looks for willing ears to hear his or her story. Nothing discourages a gossiper than not having a willing set of ears to listen. A gossiper does not want to be known as the perpetrator of the information and as a result the gossiper wants anonymity regarding the information being given out to others. In most cases the gossiper even seeks confidentiality from his/her hearer(s) because the gossiper does not want the source of the unauthorized information to be traced to him or her. Gossipers are cowards and are not up to facing the one or the group about whom they are gossiping. In order words all gossipers want to do is sneak around revealing others' information to those who have no reason to know and who could not offer any assistance to the one or group being targeted. Gossipers do not care about the consequences of their behavior to the one or group about whom they are gossiping. The gossipers only care about satisfying their own ego and making themselves look better than the one or group about which they are gossiping. What do gossipers get from gossiping? Gossiping, especially at work might result from the feelings that a staff member is not doing his or her work as well or as much as expected. If other staff members feel that the staff is getting away without consequence for a mediocre job, there could be gossiping about the staff. The staff doing the gossiping might be doing it to make himself/herself look better, it might be a way of elevating himself or herself above the other staff. Gossipers might be trying to fill the void of lack of information. When information is not readily available there could be someone who passes around information which might not be factual to appear as being in the know. Jealousy might lead the gossiper to pass around information to damage another person or the group. A gossiper might feel that gossiping would increase the gossiper's sense of belonging to the group through his or her provision of fresh information regularly. Gossipers are always in need of those who are receptive to their information. However, 'it takes two to tangle,' in other words, without the willing ears gossiping could not survive. What are the effects of gossiping in relationship? The Bible does not have anything good to say about gossiping or gossipers. "A gossip betrays a confidence, but a trustworthy person keeps a secret" (Proverbs 11: 13, NASB). "Without wood a fire goes out; without a gossip a quarrel dies down" (Proverb 26: 20, NASB). "A perverse person stirs up conflict, and a gossip separates close friends" (Proverbs 16: 20, NASB). "A false witness will not go unpunished and whoever pours out lies will not go free" (Proverbs 19: 5, NASB). Gossiping brings about contention in relationships and it separates friends. Gossiping promotes hatred between people and reduces trust. It removes confidence in others and promotes suspicion. As a result of the evil effects of gossiping it is an abomination to God. Therefore, people, especially, Christians should avoid any association which promotes gossiping. As a result of God's dislike for sin what should be the believers' response be to gossipers? Since gossiping is a sin like any other sin it is important to refer to how God expects believers to respond to sinners with the understanding that all have sinned and fall short of the Glory of God. Based on this Biblical principle, believers are not to shun away gossipers, but not to participate in the gossiping act with them. "And do not be conformed to this world, but be transformed by the renewing of your mind, so that you may prove what the will of God is, that which is good and acceptable and perfect" (Romans 12:2). Gossipers should know by the believers' examples that they are not receptive to gossiping. Gossipers like to get those with open ears to gossiping to be involved with them in their act, however, once gossipers realize that an individual is not interested in participating in gossiping, they will abstain from getting the individual involved. Believers by their daily examples should not be a fertile ground for gossipers. What is your response to a gossiper? If you demonstrate a positive response to a gossiper at the first instance you become a fertile ground for the gossiper, however, if your response does not appear to make you a fertile land for the gossiper, he/she would hunt for a fertile land somewhere else to plant his/her dangerous habit and leave you alone. Therefore, your initial response to a gossiper will either make you become his gossiping crew or not. "Let's hold firmly to the confession of our hope without wavering, for He who promised is faithful; and let's consider how to encourage one another in love and good deeds" (Hebrew 10: 23 – 24, NASB). As true followers of God your response should show the love of God and dissuade a gossiper from getting you involved in gossiping. Always ask God to lead you in your response to people who gossip because your response could make a difference.

Responses Elicited by WHY

The word WHY is a word which should be used with caution - the word why could lead others to defense - it is a challenging word which could bring the worst out of people. If someone asks another person, why did or did you not do such and such a thing? That question could be considered by the receiver as a challenge, as questioning, and/or implying that the receiver is wrong to have done what the receiver did. However, another receiver might take it as a question seeking an answer for the receiver's action. How each of both receivers perceives the intent of the questioner could determine the emotional reaction elicited/displayed and the type of responses provided by each. Previous experiences with the speaker by the receiver also could determine the type of emotion or response elicited. In a precarious relationship where there is no trust and everyone is watching the word of the other, it is advisable to avoid using any statement with 'why.' A reasonable guess of responses which the statement with 'why' could elicit fall into two categories which are either positive or negative. Positive responses could fall into about fifty-fifty percent (50%/50%) of the times they are used. The relationship between the speaker and the receiver could determine the feelings associated with the question using 'why.' The question with the word 'why' could be used to collect information, however, it might be better to rephrase the statement to get the same information without appearing to be confrontational. There are about five hundred and eleven (511) statements in the Bible which asks or makes statements using 'why' and about three hundred and sixty-seven (367) in the Old Testament and about one hundred and forty-four (144) times in the New Testament (Youversion.com). When Cain was angry with Abel God asked him, "Then the LORD said to Cain, "Why are you angry? Why is your face downcast?" (Genesis 4: 6, NIV). There are some other places in the Bible where God used 'why' in calling the attention of people to the wrong they have done or were planning to do. The use of the question why by God might be intended to let the people know that He is aware of the wrong they were planning to do or have done. Jesus used the question in giving confidence to His disciples. "…They were startled and frightened, thinking they saw a ghost. He said to them, 'Why' are you troubled, and why do doubts rise in your minds? Look at my hands and my feet. It is I myself! Touch me and see; a ghost does not have flesh and bones, as you see I have" (Luke 24: 37- 39, NIV). There was another time when Jesus used similar statement or question with God. After Jesus had carried the sins of humankind on Himself on the cross it was unpleasurable for God to look at Him as before He bore the sins of the world. Jesus instantaneously felt that God had turned His eyes away from Him momentarily Jesus then made a statement to God and asked saying, "ELI, ELI, LEMA SABAKTANEI?" that is, "MY GOD, MY GOD, WHY HAVE YOU FORSAKEN ME?" (Matthew 27: 45, NASB). In this instance Jesus was not questioning God, but He was seeking the companion of God to go through the physical agony He was experiencing from the heavy weight of the sins of the world that He was bearing on the cross. There are several purposes in the statement when the word 'why' is used in the Bible. Here are some purposes for its use in the Bible; for gathering information, obtaining reason for action, confrontational, challenging, questioning, introspection, and double checking.

Gathering Information

"But the chief priests and the elders persuaded the crowd to ask for Barabbas and to have Jesus executed. Which of the two do you want me to release to you? asked the governor. Barabbas, they answered. What shall I do, then, with Jesus who is called the Messiah?" Pilate asked. They all answered, Crucify him, Why? What crime has he committed? asked Pilate" (Matthew 20: 21 – 23, NIV). Based on the information Pilate had heard about Jesus he felt that He had not committed any offense deserving death, Pilate could have released Jesus at that point, but he left the decision for the people to make because he was concerned about his position, and he wanted to please the people. He was hoping that the people would change their minds and have Jesus released, but unfortunately with the pressure from the chief priest and the elders the people maintained their demand to have Jesus who was innocent crucified and to release Barabbas, a criminal. Pilate was not pleased with their decision and posted a question to them seeking information about what Jesus had done wrong for them to arrive at their conclusion. His questioning of 'why' elicited rage in them and they cried with a loud voice demanding that Jesus be crucified.

Obtaining Reason for an Action or for Failure to Act

The disciples at times wanted to get the information or an answer from Jesus for the reason He engaged in a method of teaching. One such example was when they asked Him, "And the disciples came up and said to Him, 'Why' do You speak to them in parables? And Jesus answered them, To you it has been granted to know the mysteries of the kingdom of heaven, but to them it has not been granted. (Matthew 13: 10, NASB). Another was the occasion of a boy whose father took him to the disciples to cast out demon out of him, but the disciples were unable. The demon disregarded the disciples command to go out of the boy. The father, therefore, took the boy to Jesus to help because His disciples were unable. Jesus cured the boy of his demon possession. Then after the whole incident was over the disciples wanted to know the reason that they were not able to cure the boy of his demon possession. They must have been very embarrassed; therefore, they went to Jesus privately away from the hearing of those who were not in their group and inquired of Jesus for the reason the demon did not obey their command to get out of the boy. "When they came to the crowd, a man came up to Jesus, falling on his knees before Him and saying, Lord, have mercy on my son, because he has seizures and suffers terribly; for he often falls into the fire and often into the water. And I brought him to Your disciples, and they could not cure him. …Bring him here to Me. And Jesus rebuked him, and the demon came out of him, and the boy was

229

healed at once. Then the disciples came to Jesus privately and said, 'Why' could we not cast it out? And He said to them, Because of your meager faith; for truly I say to you, if you have faith the size of a mustard seed, you will say to this mountain, Move from here to there, and it will move; and nothing will be impossible for you" (Matthew 17: 14 – 20). The disciples got over their embarrassment, put up courage and asked Jesus for the reason that they failed, and Jesus told them the reason the demon did not listen to them was because their faith was very small, even smaller than a mustard seed.

Confrontational

The pharisees were very antagonistic to Jesus and they always looked for opportunity to catch Him or His disciples in doing what they perceived to be sinful. In one of many occasions, they confronted Jesus regarding the wrong they felt that His disciples did. "One Sabbath Jesus was going through the grainfields, and as his disciples walked along, they began to pick some heads of grain. The Pharisees said to him, Look, 'why' are they doing what is unlawful on the Sabbath?" (Mark 2: 23 – 24). The pharisees' intention was not to seek answers but to confront Jesus.

Challenging

"Then the Pharisees went out and laid plans to trap him in his words. They sent their disciples to him along with the Herodians. Teacher, they said, we know that you are a man of integrity and that you teach the way of God in accordance with the truth. You aren't swayed by others because you pay no attention to who they are. Tell us then, what is your opinion? Is it right to pay the imperial tax to Caesar or not? But Jesus, knowing their evil intent, said, You hypocrites, 'why' are you trying to trap me?" (Matthew 22: 14 – 17., NIV). Whenever someone comes to you with excessive praise it is either the person or group wants a favor from you, or they want to set you up for failure, or they want to use your words against you in a future accusation. Therefore, whenever you experience such flattery be watchful of what you do or say in response because it could be used against you. So, allow God to give you directions on how to respond on those situations. This was the case with Jesus when the Pharisees and their collaborators were trying to catch Him with His words. What they wanted Jesus to say was that they were not to pay taxes to Caesar, however, since Jesus knew their motives, He was able to respond to them appropriately. Jesus confronted them of their intent to trap Him and their scheme failed.

Questioning

Cain and Abel were the first two brothers of the same parents. Abel kept flocks, and Cain was a farmer. Cain and Abel brought their individual offering to the Lord, Cain from his farm product and Abel from his flock. Cain did not bring the best of the product of his fam as an offering to the Lord, however, Abel brought the best of his flock as an offering to the Lord. The Lord was pleased with Abel's offering, but Cain's offering was repugnant to the Lord. Cain became angry and the Lord asked him why he was angry with his brother. The Lord warned him that he needed to put his anger under control, otherwise, it would become a sin against him. The Lord asked Cain the question 'why' to make him realize that it was not Abel's fault that his offering was not accepted, but that it was due to the quality of his offering (Genesis 4: 2 – 7, NIV).

Introspection

When Job was going through the problems with the loss of his possessions and his family at certain times in his suffering he complained to God. However, he looked inwardly and uttered this statement in response to his friends who were tormenting him. "As for me, is my complaint to a mortal? Or 'why' should I not be impatient?" (Job 21: 4, NASB). Job felt that he should not allow the tormenting of his friends make him to be inpatient with God.

Clarification

When a ruler came to Jesus and called Him Good Teacher, Jesus did not want to ascribe that glory to Himself, and He wanted the ruler to know that only God is good. This clarification is a testament to the humanity of Christ indicating that no human is good. "A ruler questioned Him, saying, Good Teacher, what shall I do to inherit eternal life? But Jesus said to him, 'Why' do you call Me good? No one is good except God alone" (Luke 18: 18 – 19, NASB).

Response to Disappointment

It is always difficult to accept disappointment, especially, when it comes from areas or from the person(s) one does not expect it. When Jesus was disappointed by His trusted treasurer who betrayed Him, how did he respond? While dying on the cross Jesus prayed to God to forgive the one who betrayed him, those who condemned Him to death, and those who crucified Him by asking the Father to forgive them because they did not know what they were doing. In His death Jesus was still giving the benefit of the doubt to those who treated Him unkindly by saying that they did not know what they were doing. Have you ever given the benefit of the doubt to anyone you felt has disappointed you or who has treated you badly in any situation? This is a rhetorical question for you to measure your responses to that of Jesus and see where you are on the scale which Jesus has set by His responses. Paul stated, "Humble yourselves, therefore, under God's mighty hand that He may lift you up in due time. Cast your anxiety on Him because He cares for you" (1 Peter 5: 6 – 7). Disappointment is a humbling experience to humans, however, Paul's piece of advice that believers should humble themselves before God in addition to the humbling experience from humans is gut ranching. The humbling experience from humans is forced on the believers, but the humbling experience before God is voluntary. Through the voluntary humbleness under the mighty power of God comes God's uplifting of believers before long, at the right time. The Lord will remove all anxieties associated with the disappointment if believers give over their anxiety to Him and leave it at the feet of the cross. Job must have been disappointed for all the evils which befell him. When everything he had perished, he showed his human emotion, but he quickly got over his emotion and worshipped God (Job 1: 20 – 22; 13: 15a, NASB). As a result of Job's humbleness and service to God, God comforted him and upheld him in his grief, sorrow, loss, and sufferings. Although his friends disappointed him, he did not retaliate against them, but he left all judgement to God. The Psalmist said, "…The angel of the Lord encamps around those who fear Him, and He delivers them (Psalm 34: 1 – 7, NASB). It has been commonly said that 'with every disappointment there is a blessing in disguise.' This is true if only humans will be patient and seek the face of God and listen to God's speaking quietly to them regarding how things do happen, sometimes, the way they happen. The one going through disappointment might be too overwhelmed to see the hand of God, but with humbleness of heart God will reveal Himself in the disappointment. Paul states, "Therefore, since we have been justified by faith, we have peace with God through our Lord Jesus Christ, through whom we have gained access by faith into His grace in which we now stand. And we boast in the hope of the glory of God. Not only so, but we also glory in our sufferings because we know that suffering produces perseverance; perseverance character; and character hope. And hope does not put us to shame because God's love has been poured out into our hearts through the Holy Spirit who has been given to us" (Romans 5: 3 – 5, NASB). Disappointments could lead to suffering; however, Paul encourages believers that suffering might not be in vain because if one endures the suffering it could lead to character development. Just as athletes go through the rigor of suffering and the pain of practice which lead them into character for endurance, so is faith in God during suffering. As the athletes' suffering produces endurance leads them with the hope that they are ready to compete and win. Such hope does not fail because it produces strength in the athletes to win, in order words, it becomes a self-fulfilling prophesy for winning. In Paul's writing he was using an athletic metaphor. Paul's statement points to the fact that the believers hope in God will never fail and all disappointments along the way could lead to a more reliance on God to carry out His purpose in the disappointment. Habakkuk states, "For the revelation awaits an appointed time, it speaks of the end and will not prove false. Though it lingers, wait for it; it will certainly come and will not delay" (Habakkuk 2: 3, NASB). Habakkuk's statement is in line with Paul's statement confirming that believers need to be patient and wait on the Lord even though the fulfilment of God's rescue appears to be delayed it will never fail. The lyric of the song below is very appropriate for patience with the Lord.

> *There's not a mountain too tall*
> *There's not a problem too small*
> *That Jesus can't resolve*
> *In time He'll get involved*
> *Our God He cares about us*
> *So wait on the Lord*
> *Wait on the Lord*
> *Wait on the Lord*
> *And He'll renew your strength*
> *There's not a light too dark*
> *A journey too long to embark*
> *Jesus will see you through*
> *In time He'll make you new*
> *Our God He cares about us*
> *So wait on the Lord*
> *Wait on the Lord*
> *Wait on the Lord*
> *And He'll renew your strength*
> *'Cause He's ordering, He's ordering your strength*
> *You've got to wait, you've got to wait*
> (James Wilson / Natalie Bunne).

God expects believers to trust Him that He always stands by his word that He will never forsake all who have their trust in Him. God expects Christians to keep hope alive. "Be joyful in hope, patient in affliction, faithful in prayer" (Romans 12: 12, NASB). There was a saying in some Christian circles while talking about prayer, here is how the saying goes, 'is prayer your steering wheel or your spare tire?' This is a question that a Christian should answer honestly to themselves because God knows the answer. The point is, is prayer what you apply regularly or as needed? The answer is between you and God and depending on your answer He will convict you of the right step to take. Remember that prayer is the ladder which leads to God, it is a Christian's connective tissue to God. "The Lord will fight for you; you only need to be still" Exodus 14: 14, NASB). "Yet the Lord longs to be gracious to you; therefore, he will rise up to

235

show you compassion. For the Lord is a God of justice. Blessed are all who wait for him (Isaiah 30: 18, NASB). The above is the promise of God to the Israelites on their way to the promised land. The promise for the Israelites then is still applicable to Christians today and Christians should remember when disappointments hit that God will fight for them, however, He expects them to be still. Isaiah continued similar pieces of advice, even after the Israelites journey was over by encouraging them to wait on the Lord because the Lord longs to show them grace and to be compassionate to them. Isaiah was pleading for their patience for the Lord. "But, do not forget this one thing, dear friends: With the Lord a day is like a thousand years, and a thousand years are like a day. The Lord is not slow in keeping His promise, as some understand slowness. Instead, he is patient with you, not wanting anyone to perish, but to come into repentance (2 Peter 3: 8 – 9, NASB). Many times, people wonder why God has not struck down all evil doers or why they have not seen any evil befall those who have disappointed them. Whenever Christians have such mindset, they need to refer to the words of Peter to the Christians and glean the reasons from the pages of the Bible for the reason God has not paid them evil for the wrong they have done. The Lord is a God of patience to give people ample chance to repent of their evil ways and be saved. God has similar patience to those who have accepted Him and those who have not accepted Him. "For it is by grace you have been saved, through faith – and this is not from yourselves, it is the gift of God, so that no one can boast" (Ephesians 2: 8, NASB). Christians are admonished to remember that they were saved only by the grace of God and as a result should never look at people as deserving punishment for the sins they have committed because all have sinned including the Christians and it is only through the grace provided by God that they were saved. When the young rich man went to Jesus trying to prove himself to be righteous in keeping the laws and believing that his work has made him good enough to enter the kingdom of God. Jesus pointed to him in a subtle way that his goodness could never be good enough to earn the grace of God, but his love for God and for his fellow humans. The rich young man quickly realized that he was not good enough and he went away sorrowfully abandoning the Kingdom of God (Matthew

19: 16 – 25). Disappointment generally comes from those who are friends, close acquaintances, associates, or even from family members. Disappointments usually comes from those one least expects them and that is one of the reasons that disappointment hit one to the core. There was a man who was a realtor by trade. Information about his occupation was known to his close friends, family members, and acquaintances. He was not a quiet realtor because he let all know about his trade and how he could be of assistance to them with buying or selling their houses or land properties. He was fully confident, because of his relationship with those people, that he would be the person they would approach for their real estate needs. There was a single elderly woman whose children live several miles away from her, but in the same state. She became a trusted family friend of the realtor. The realtor's family members know her well and she knows them well. She trusted the realtor and she relied on getting financial pieces of advice from him including information needed to sell her house. The realtor got comparative market analysis of how much houses have been selling in her neighborhood. She even invited the realtor to her house to tell her what she could do to get the most price for her house. The realtor went to assess her house and he recommended some things to improve her house for sale. Since this woman has been a family friend for such a long time and since she has been seeking pieces of advice from the realtor, the realtor assumed that he would be the one to sell the woman's house. The woman began to park her belongings into boxes to be ready for the sale of her house. The sale of the house appeared eminent; therefore, the realtor friend asked the woman over the phone as to when she would want him to put her house in the market for sale. To the surprise of the realtor, the woman responded that when she bought her house about fifteen (15) years ago she told the realtor who assisted her to buy the house that she would be the one who would assist her to sell it when the time comes. The realtor was very surprised and felt used by the woman to get all appropriate information to sell her house without disclosing to the realtor that she had someone else she intended to assist her to sell the house. The realtor was quiet, not knowing how to respond and he was searching for words to use in order not to destroy their relationship. The realtor said, "is there any reason you are not having me assist you to sell your house?" To which the woman responded, "I have known her for about fifteen (15) years." The realtor responded by saying, "but you have known me for longer." The woman then responded, "Are we still friends" The realtor responded, "yes, we are still friends and if you need my assistance any time, let me know. It was not meant for me to assist you to sell your house, but God will provide some other people who will need my assistance to sell or buy houses." They ended the conversation without any visible anger from the realtor. However, the realtor was very disappointed and could not believe what had just happened. He told his wife who was also surprised that the woman could do such a thing after using the realtor to gather all the information she needed. Not long after the conversation, the woman called the realtor requesting the realtor's son to take pictures of her belongings which she wanted to sell. The realtor told his son who readily agreed to assist the woman. The realtor drove his son to the woman's house and his son took all the pictures of the belongings which the woman wanted to sell and posted them online. The woman showed her gratitude for the assistance. The woman still called the realtor, thereafter for assistance as needed and the realtor continued to render her assistance. One day when the realtor was not around, the realtor's wife told their son who took and posted the pictures online that the woman gave the sale of her house to another realtor. The son was very surprised and told her mother that his father never mentioned that to him. The son asked the father at the first opportunity he had about the fact that the woman gave her house to another realtor to sell. The father confirmed the information as being true. The son then asked, "why are we still helping her then?" The father saw this as a teaching moment and a time to demonstrate a Christian example as to what being a Christian means, which is, do not pay evil for evil as Jesus taught. The father (realtor) referred his son to the teaching of Jesus. "Give to everyone who asks of you, and whoever takes away what is yours, do not demand it back. Treat people the same way you want them to treat you. If you love those who love you, what credit is that to you? For even sinners love those who love them. And if you do good to those who do good to you, what credit is that to you? For even sinners do the same. And if you lend to those from whom you expect to receive, what credit is that to you? Even sinners lend to sinners in order to receive back the same amount. But love your enemies and do good, and lend, expecting nothing in return; and your reward will be great, and you will be sons of the Most High; for He Himself is kind to ungrateful and evil people. Be merciful, just as your Father is merciful" (Luke 6: 30 – 36, NASB). This situation gave the realtor (the father) an opportune time to show his son the reason he continued to assist the woman with the sale of her house even though she gave it to someone else to sell. The son learnt a great lesson from the incident regarding the appropriate way for Christians to respond to disappointments. The realtor's response most likey have planted a seed in the life of the son which would become a giant tree in the Kingdom of God. Remember that your responses could make a difference in your life, in your relationship with humans and with God, and in your relationship to the unbelievers, therefore, stay steadfast with God and follow his principles and examples in your dealings with others even if they have done you wrong. Remember how much wrong you do to God every day or to His creations and He still loves you, therefore, reciprocate similar love to others.

Response in Flexibility

In life things cannot and will not always go ones' own way or as expected. There are always surprises around the corner in life. However, outcome to every situation or issue depends on how one responds to it. When one responds to issue(s) with flexibility the outcome could be positive, however, if one responds to issues with rigidity the result might be less pleasing, or it might be tragic. Taking an example from the palm trees and the regular trees. Palm trees do not readily break or fall during fierce stormy winds as regular trees do because they are flexible enough to bend in the direction of the wind. Trees on the other hand are more rigid than palm trees and they often fall than palm trees do. People who are flexible are prone to be happier and maintain healthy relationships than people who are rigid. Flexibility is a word which could be interchanged with the word change. In order to accept any change an individual has to be flexible. In this modern age changes come fast and furious than one could recover from prior changes, but only those who are flexible to changes could survive, thrive, and advance. Individuals, companies, or organizations who or which are rigid or inflexible could not survive or thrive in the constantly changing environment. God showed His flexibility in dealing with human beings. There are several occasions in the Bible whereby God demonstrated His flexibility in dealing with humans. Some examples will be discussed here. When the sins of the people of Sodom and Gomorrah rose up to the Lord, He decided to destroy them, however, Abraham intervened and pleaded with the Lord. Abraham respectively negotiated with God. Abraham 'tested the water' with God by proposing to God if God would not destroy the cities of Sodom and Gomorrah if certain numbers of righteous people were found in the cities. Abraham started with a high number of fifty righteous people, and he asked God if He would spare the cities on the account of finding fifty righteous people. In cities of thousands of people, to be hoping to find fifty righteous people was quite insignificant with human standards, but with God one person is significant. In the flexibility of God, He agreed to safe the cities of thousands on the account of finding fifty righteous ones. Abraham was not sure if there could be fifty righteous people in cities of thousands of people, therefore, he reduced his expectation and request of God from fifty righteous people to forty-five righteous people in both cities. In reducing the number of his request Abraham was very apologetic to God. God went along with the idea of not destroying the cities if forty-five righteous people were found in both cities. Abraham did not stop with his request of getting forty-five righteous people in both cities, but he reduced the number of righteous people to be found in both cities to forty. God in His mercy still agreed not to destroy Sodom and Gomorrah if forty righteous people were found in both cities. Abraham felt that he had been pushing his luck to the limit with God and for that he sought God's forgiveness, but he continued his requests. He then requested of the Lord if He would not destroy the cities if there were only thirty righteous people in the cities. God was very amenable to Abraham's request and God assured Abraham that He would not destroy the cities for the sake of thirty righteous people. Abraham continued to press for the least number of the righteous people on behalf of which the Lord would have mercy on the cities. Abraham put up courage to ask God again and he must be thinking that God would eventually get upset with him. Abraham made another request of the Lord the Lord if He would not destroy the cities if only twenty righteous people were found in them. However, to Abraham's surprise God was merciful enough to determine not to destroy the cities for the sake of only twenty righteous people in them. Abraham did not stop his requests with the amazing flexibility of God in accepting his requests, thus far, but he became respectively emboldened and made more requests. Abraham reduced his request of finding righteous people in Sodom and Gomorrah to one half of his last request by asking the Lord if He would spare the cities from destruction if only ten righteous people were found in the cities. God demonstrated His wish for no one to perish, but for everyone to come to repentance. Therefore, God was patient with Abraham with his endless requests and pleas. God was very flexible in His response and accommodation of Abraham (Genesis 18: 24 – 33). The Israelites provoked the Lord after the visit of the twelve spies to the land of Canaan by doubting God's ability to save them. They doubted God to keep His promise to them that He would give them the land of Canaan which was flowing with milk and honey for a possession. God was disappointed with them and was ready to destroy them. Moses was instrumental in appeasing God on behalf of the Israelites and God was flexible in His response to the plea of Moses and he relented in destroying the Israelites at once. On another occasion when Aaron made a golden calf for the people and thus led them to worship the idol he created for them God was very upset with them and was determined to destroy them. Moses intervened again and God listened to Moses on behalf of the Israelites. God showed His flexibility again and spared the lives of the Israelites despite their rebellion against Him. God has always been mindful of His creation, but He hated sin, but humans are prone to sinning. God devised means for the atonement of their sins through the sacrifice of animals and birds. The sacrifice of animals and birds was not good as a permanent remedy for human sins, therefore, other solution for repeated sacrifices of animals and birds was to be provided. God in a flexible provision sent Jesus to die once for the sins of all humanity throughout the entire universe. This final act of flexibility by God was and is the final hope of eternity for humans. Are you easy to talk with or difficult to approach? What is your relationship with your spouse, friends, children, family, coworkers, subordinates, superiors, members of your group, associates, and acquaintances? Must you have the last say in every conversation and must your words be the only words that must 'carry the day' (be followed)? Are you in the habit of, it is only either your way or the highway? If this is you, then you need to have an introspection of yourself (examine yourself inwardly) and ask God to renew your heart. Since God has demonstrated His flexibility throughout history how flexibly are your response to God's call for you? When all efforts to appease God failed, in His flexibility He provided a sure way of salvation to all humans by sending Christ as the final sacrifice to save all who take advantage of His flexibility. Paul declared the eagerness of God to safe sinners in the following sayings: "And working together with Him, we also urge you not to receive the grace of God in vain— for He says at the acceptable time I listened to you, And on the day of salvation I helped you. Behold, now is the acceptable time behold, now is the day of salvation" (2 Corinthians 6: 1 – 3, NASB). Are you flexible enough to accept the provision of God for your salvation? Jesus has taken the first step to save you, now it is your turn to take the next step towards Him for your salvation. Be flexible to bend His ways and receive the salvation which is waiting for you to claim. Your response to Him could make a difference in where you spend eternity.

Conclusion

This book gives non-exhaustive synopsis of examples of people group, individuals, and nations to the issues which confronted them, how they responded and what the effects of their responses were on themselves, on their families, on their nations, and on the world. Above all, it shows some of the ways God responded and continues to respond to how His creatures rsresponded, are responding, or should be responding to Him. Through God's dealings with humans He was and still is true to His words. Many times, God relented in the way He delt and is dealing with human beings. There were and still are times when humans pushed/push God's patience to the limit and from there on, He was committed never to destroy His creation again. Although the Israelites deserved harsher punishment for their lack of believe and trust in God, God was very merciful unto them because of His promise to Abraham and the intervention of Moses. As a leader one needs to keep one's eyes on the Lord and not allow the frustration from the followers to disrupt one's relationship with the Lord. Being disobedient to the Lord in one's response to Him has adverse consequences as noted in the responses of Adam and Eve, Pharaoh, and Jonah. After reading this book, ponder on what God is requesting of you. The time of ignorance is over. You might think that you have not heard the word of God speaking to you, however, that is not true because God continues to speak to people in many ways and through daily situations only if they pay attention and listen could they hear God speaking.

"The heavens tell of the glory of God;
And their expanse declares the work of His hands.
Day to day pours forth speech,
And night to night reveals knowledge.
There is no speech, nor are there words;
Their voice is not heard.
Their line has gone out into all the earth,

And their words to the end of the world.
In them He has placed a tent for the sun,
Which is like a groom coming out of his chamber;
It rejoices like a strong person to run his course.
Its rising is from one end of the heavens,
And its circuit to the other end of them;
And there is nothing hidden from its heat" (Psalm 19: 1-6, NASB).

There was the story of a man who was driving in a drizzling rain, and he got to a traffic stop light and had to stop for the light to turn green for him to go. As he was waiting for the traffic light to change, he noticed some small birds moving frantically around picking at something on the ground . Suddenly one of them was successful in finding a worm which it dragged out of its burrow and swallowed it.

The man was very impressed on how God provided food for the little bird in the middle of nowhere on the lawn. The man felt that God was speaking to him by allowing him to be at the right place at the right time for the traffic light to turn red as he was approaching the intersection where he had to stop to see God's provision for the little bird. He praised God because the incident spoke to him that God who provided for the bird of the air would meet his needs and that he should cast all his burdens on Him. "…because that which is known about God is evident within them; for God made it evident to them. For since the creation of the world His invisible attributes, that is, His eternal power and divine nature, have been clearly perceived, being understood by what has been made, so that they are without

245

excuse. For even though they knew God, they did not honor Him as God or give thanks, but they became futile in their reasonings, and their senseless hearts were darkened" (Romans 1: 19 – 21, NASB).

Looking at nature, the sun, the moon, the light, the darkness, the desert, the hills, the mountains, the oceans, the rivers, the rain, the sky, the mountains, and the valleys all point to the marvelous provision of God. All His creation speak for Him only if human beings would stop and ponder on the wonderful work He has done. All those creations speak to human beings constantly about God. What is your response when you observe all the creative action of God and His provision for all? Your response is an indication of your allegiance either to God or to the devil. If your response to God in anything is, YES Lord, send me send me, then your allegiance is to God, but if your response to God is, NO, send someone else, then your allegiance is, or could be to the devil. It is important, however, to know that each of your responses has consequence(s). As you have just read some examples of consequences to people's or nations' responses in this book, consider that how you respond to Christ is dependent on your trust in Him, how you believe His words, His promise, His cleansing power, and His power to save. Note the lyric of this hymn:

'Tis so sweet to trust in Jesus,
Just to take Him at His Word
Just to rest upon His promise,
Just to know, "Thus saith the Lord!"
Jesus, Jesus, how I trust Him!

How I've proved Him o'er and o'er
Jesus, Jesus, precious Jesus!
Oh, for grace to trust Him more!
I'm so glad I learned to trust Him,
Precious Jesus, Savior, Friend
And I know that He is with me,
Will be with me to the end.
Oh, how sweet to trust in Jesus,
Just to trust His cleansing blood
And in simple faith to plunge me
'Neath the healing, cleansing flood!
Yes, 'tis sweet to trust in Jesus,
Just from sin and self to cease
Just from Jesus simply taking
Life and rest, and joy and peace.
(Canzetta Staton / Louisa M. Stead / William James Kirkpatrick).

Your response could bring blessings and happiness to you from the Lord or curse and unhappiness from the devil, therefore, weigh how you respond to God. The consequences of your response could be marvelous reward of spending eternity with God in heaven or spending a miserable eternity with the devil in hell. Remember that your response has consequences with people and more importantly with God, therefore, ponder and make the best response towards God. May God direct and bless you as your respond positively to Him.

www.ingramcontent.com/pod-product-compliance
Lightning Source LLC
Chambersburg PA
CBHW051302120626
46547CB00015B/2057